PUB W
IN
Leicestershire & Rutland

THIRTY CIRCULAR WALKS
AROUND LEICESTERSHIRE
& RUTLAND INNS

Bryan Waites

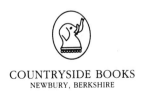

COUNTRYSIDE BOOKS
NEWBURY, BERKSHIRE

Photographs by Beryl Waites
Maps by author
Cover design by Mon Mohan
Cover illustration by Colin Doggett

Produced through MRM Associates Ltd., Reading
Typeset by Paragon Typesetters, Queensferry, Clwyd
Printed in England

Dedicated
To
'Our Ivy'
Loved and Remembered Always

Contents

Publisher's Note

We hope that you obtain considerable enjoyment from this book; great care has been taken in its preparation. However, changes of landlord and actual closures are sadly not uncommon. Likewise, although at the time of publication all routes followed public rights of way or well-established permitted paths, diversion orders can be made and permissions withdrawn.

We cannot accept responsibility for any inaccuracies, but we are anxious that all details covering both pubs and walks are kept up to date, and would therefore welcome information from readers which would be relevant to future editions.

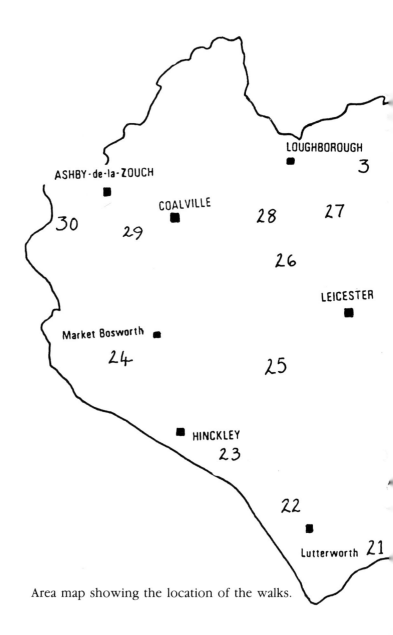

Area map showing the location of the walks.

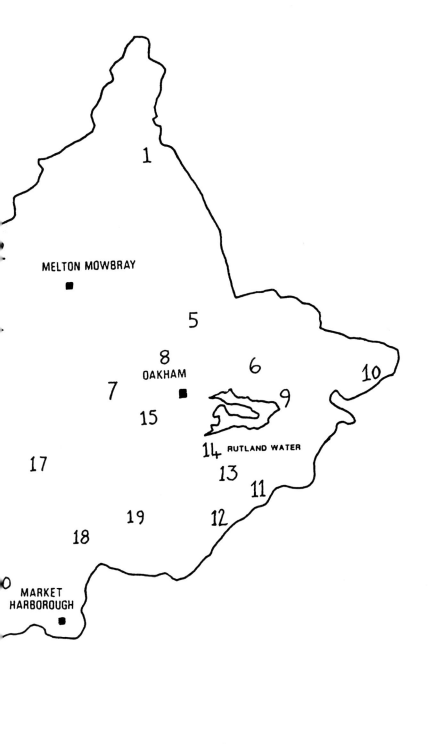

MELTON MOWBRAY

1

5

8
OAKHAM

6

10

7

9

15

14 RUTLAND WATER

17

13

11

19

12

18

MARKET
HARBOROUGH

Introduction

Leicestershire and Rutland is, upon investigation, as classic an area for pubs and scenery as the Chilterns, the Cotswolds and the West Country, and, after reading this book and walking the routes, I think you will be amazed at the diversity, interest and secrets revealed.

The selection of 30 walks represents the surprisingly varied countryside of the county that has the city of Leicester at its very centre. The choice caused much heart-searching. As always, there is a tendency for good scenery and good pubs to concentrate, in this case in the rolling hills of the east and in the Charnwood Forest area. My aim has been to reconcile a good pub and a good walk. Some pubs have been omitted because the rights of way were few or discontinuous around them. Sometimes a really splendid walk lacked a good pub. Often, there was an abundance of riches in one village where several excellent pubs were available but I had to choose only one – invidious!

The walks vary between 2 and 5½ miles and offer a variety of scenery from the Vale of Belvoir to the river Soar floodplain; from Rutland Water to the quarry at Stoney Cove. The length of the walks should suit all the family and they are usually close to other attractions which you might visit during the day, for most of the walks can be done in one session, either morning or afternoon.

Whilst I have made every effort to be accurate, please be ready for changes at the pubs which may lead to new decor, new times, different food. Also, though we mostly know about 'usual' drinking hours, these vary even in the 30 chosen pubs, so look carefully at the entry. Telephone numbers are included so that you can consult the landlord, in advance if you deem it useful and necessary, especially about leaving your car whilst on the walk, or about dogs and children. I have given helpful information about these matters where I can, but it might be wise to double-check.

Even the most accommodating of landlords is unlikely to welcome walkers with muddy boots and wellingtons, so please leave yours outside or change in the car. You should use discretion about eating your own food on the premises even when you buy a drink. Many landlords allow this, but I think they may be reluctant even whilst being co-operative. Why not also buy a snack or even a meal and turn your day into one of real pleasure?

Depending on the season in which you walk you will find variations in terrain, but always be prepared for muddy walks in parts as this is an area of heavy clay, at least in the west, often near watermeadows, along bridleways or across fields. Occasionally, you may have to walk over a ploughed field if that is the right of way, unless you can get round the edge successfully. Remember the Countryside Code at all times, and treat the landscape with respect.

Leicestershire County Council in association with the Countryside Commission have launched a 'Waymark 2000 Project' to signpost 3,000 miles of footpaths and public rights of way by the year 2000. This is a big task and I must say, in many miles of walking, there is a great deal still to do. Hence, you will not find all the notices you need and many walks have had to be pioneered. Follow the directions in the book carefully to avoid going astray. There is also a scheme underway to map and clarify bridleways, which should bring results in a few years' time. Additionally, I have been glad to consult the publications of the Leicestershire Footpath Association's *Leicestershire Round*, the helpful books of Heather MacDermid, and the *Leicester Mercury Walks* as well as the numerous local parish walks available.

CAMRA won its fight for real ale as visits to many of these pubs will show. Now it is in a new fight to save the traditional pub and to protect its character, especially those with buildings of historic and architectural value. This campaign was launched as the *Manifesto for Pub Preservation* which calls for customers to be consulted before changes are made. This should help to stem the danger from creeping modernisation which is threatening some pubs of character. In this book you will find real old pubs and I did not hesitate to include the ordinary local on occasions.

The British are not the leading beer drinkers. The Germans drink twice our amount. They also lead in drinking spirits and soft drinks. However, we do excel in milk-drinking. Perhaps it is this combination of milk and beer that makes us inveterate walkers. Don't forget that a pub these days does offer much more than alcohol and basic rolls. You can get all kind of drinks and, often, gourmet food, and accommodation. But why we all go in the end is because 'the inns of England are the best in Europe . . . when you have lost your inns, drown your empty selves for you will have lost the last of England' (Hilaire Belloc, *This, That and The Other)*. Village pubs are an integral part of our countryside heritage and even though they may have lost many local characters and something of their original community, they still open up to us the secrets of the rural world.

I gratefully acknowledge the help that I have received from Beryl Waites, Paul Waites, Andrew Ramshaw, Dr Gillian Dawson and Richard Drewe.

Bryan Waites

① Knipton
The Red House Inn

This 250 year old former hunting lodge stands in its own spacious gardens and overlooks the pretty village of Knipton which has the splendid sight of Belvoir Castle on the hill above. Much of the land around is still part of the Duke of Rutland's estate. Oddly enough, though Knipton and Belvoir Castle are amongst the leading attractions of Leicestershire, they are so close to Lincolnshire that the postal address is Grantham, Lincs, thus misleading visitors into believing that they actually belong to that county.

The Red House was a private residence until about 30 years ago. During and after World War II it was used for several different purposes and it may be that the ghost of a small child, seen from time to time, dates from this period. As you go through the front door you have the feeling of entering an elegant country mansion.

Inside, the large lounge is comfortable and most pleasant, with a long bar. The Hornbeams Restaurant and Conservatory is a no smoking area and there is a full menu every day for lunch and dinner ranging from the very best English to Japanese cuisine. Good value soup, baguettes and ploughman's are well supported by items such as curries with basmati rice, venison and juniper pie, and steaks.

Eating times are 12 noon-2 pm (Saturday 2.30 pm) and 7 pm-10 pm (Sunday 9 pm).

Well-kept real ales include Bath, John Smiths and changing guest ales, with Dry Blackthorn cider on draught. This freehouse can arrange hunting, shooting and coarse fishing for visitors and accommodation is available. There is a garden area for children and a beer garden. Well-behaved dogs are welcome and patrons are welcome to leave the car during their walk. Drinking times are: 11 am-3 pm on weekdays and 12 noon-3 pm on Sundays.

Telephone: Grantham (01476) 870352.

How to get there: Knipton is 10 miles north east of Melton Mowbray and 7 miles south west of Grantham. From either place take the A607 and turn off at the sign for Knipton.

Parking: There is a large, excellent car park at the Red House.

Length of the walk: 5 miles. Maps: OS Landranger series 130, Pathfinder SK 83/93 and SK 82/92 (GR 828312).

This walk is a triangular route between three contrasting villages – Knipton, Croxton Kerrial (pronounced Crowson) and Branston-By-Belvoir. Knipton lies between Belvoir Upper Lake and the Knipton Reservoir and most of the village is off the main road. It has been strongly influenced by the Belvoir Estate. Croxton Kerrial is more compact and the lighter building stone is very different from the brown marlstone used in Branston. The latter village is situated in sharply undulating landscape between two streams which, together, produce the river Devon flowing through both Knipton Reservoir and Belvoir Upper Lake, eventually reaching the old Grantham Canal and carrying on to the Trent. There are excellent views from near to Branston in the direction of the reservoir. Usually, people head for Belvoir Castle and forget the lovely villages and countryside around. The area is secret and special – you should not miss it.

The Walk

On leaving the Red House, turn right onto the road to Croxton Kerrial. Walk uphill and, as you reach the top, look back for a good view of Belvoir Castle. Soon you walk on level ground and, to your right, you will glimpse the spire of Branston church and the village, just over 1 mile away. As you enter Croxton Kerrial you pass the church which is on your left. Take some time to look round this interesting village then turn right into Chapel Lane. Walk along the lane downhill to the waterworks, which is about ½ mile from the centre of the village. Here the lane changes into a wide farm track which might be muddy

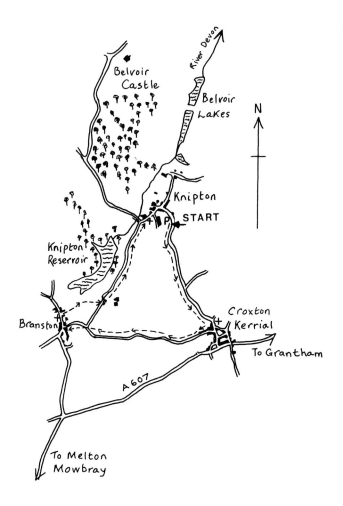

in wet weather. Follow this track as it bears left over the hill. Carry on for ¾ mile until the track reaches the Branston – Knipton road. At the road, turn left to follow this pleasant lane into Branston. Note the village quarry, now derelict, into the local marlstone, to your right.

At the Main Street, turn right past the Wheel Inn, the old school with its bell still intact on the right and, almost opposite, St Guthlac's church. Look for the bridlepath sign on the right and turn into this path between the buildings. This leads to a handgate on the left of a small paddock. Go through this gate crossing a steep-sided valley to a wide wooden gate which you can see high up on the far side. You will need to find the best place to cross the tiny stream in the valley floor. As you follow this route you have fine views of the Knipton Reservoir.

When you reach the gate on the far side of the valley (and it is quite a climb up to it) look to your left to find a handgate only a few yards away. Go through this and follow a large field all the way round its edge until it takes you to the Branston – Knipton road at cottages, formerly part of Croxton Lodge. Turn left to follow the road into Knipton, 1 mile away. At a T junction you bear right into the village. About ½ mile further on take the Croxton road which leads you back to the Red House.

Please find a little time to look around Knipton which has some very interesting features, especially off the main road. The walk can easily be combined with a visit to Belvoir Castle, only 2 miles away, which is open from early April to early October. (Telephone 0476 870262 for actual days and times.)

2 Old Dalby
The Crown Inn

Is there a harder inn to find in all England? It would seem that it was hidden away on purpose to keep the secret exclusive to just a few people. Take the trouble to seek it out – it is surely one of the country's best pubs and unique in its character. Persist, as it is difficult to locate even when you are in the lane where it is situated. Then you will find what looks like an old farmhouse. At the back is a fine terrace with a lovely garden, roses, fruit trees and tables overlooking a big lawn. A modest door seems to belong to an ordinary house, you hardly dare enter as it is so private.

Once inside, a small bar faces you, and here there is a galaxy of real ales on offer – Badger Tanglefoot, Exmoor Gold, Marston's Pedigree, Owd Roger, Ringwood Fortyniner, Woodforde's Wherry and Black Sheep, all these can be seen in cask form behind the bar. Then there are several different sized rooms just as one would find in a farmhouse, with beams galore, a cosy feel, fresh flowers in summer, open fires in winter, hunting prints, several original oak settles – indeed it is home from home. There are rotating guest beers, for example, Adnams and Bateman XXXB, well supported by 20 malt whiskies and many other mouth-watering liquors. Drinking times are 12 noon-2.30 pm and

6 pm-11 pm, Sundays 12 noon-3 pm and 7 pm-10.30 pm in this excellent freehouse.

Snacks and meals are available lunchtimes and evenings from 6 pm-10 pm, apart from Sunday evenings. They are fresh and home-made and can include such delights as oven-baked tomatoes stuffed with cheese, walnuts and sweetcorn, bumper ploughman's lunches and black pudding and fried apple in a creamy mustard sauce. There are Continental specialities also on offer. Children are welcome in eating areas and of course in the garden, but this place, despite its secret location, gets very busy at times and can become cramped for space inside. One room has games such as darts, dominoes, cribbage and table skittles. By the way, have you found the pump?

Don't miss this unique place.

Telephone: Melton Mowbray (01664) 823134.

How to get there: Old Dalby is 6 miles north west of Melton Mowbray. Follow the A6006 out of Melton and, just before reaching the A46, look for signs indicating the village which is 2 miles off to the right at Dalby Wolds. If approaching along the A46 go to Six Hills and turn off as if for Melton but then, on reaching the A6006, follow signs to Old Dalby. Go down Wood's Hill into the village. Carry on past the green and when you come to Longcliff Hill Road turn left into it. Go uphill as the road bears left past houses. Look for Debdale Hill Road on your left and turn into it. This is a narrow road easily missed. Go ahead and to the left of the building in front of you, you will see a narrow entrance to the car park of the Crown.

Parking: Excellent parking for at least 30 cars in the pub car park.

Length of the walk: 2¾ miles. Maps: OS Landranger series 129, Pathfinder SK 62/72 (GR 672239).

Old Dalby is located between two Roman roads, now the A46 and the B676. It is on the edge of the Leicestershire Wolds and the Vale of Belvoir. On the walk you can obtain glimpses of the latter beyond Nether Broughton. Its situation on a scarp results in sharply undulating hills all around, such as Longcliff and Wood's Hill. This most pleasant walk crosses the village green, passes the church and climbs to high ground above Old Dalby Wood. Then the route is through the woods back towards the church and Hall across former parkland.

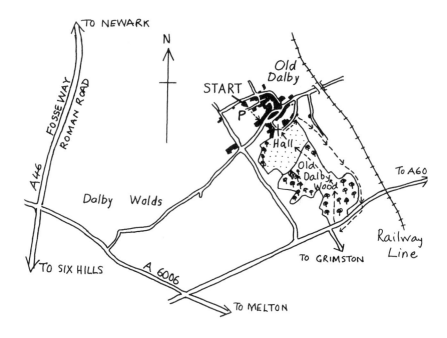

The Walk

Turn right as you come out of the pub door and go through the small wooden gate a few yards away. Close the gate and turn left along a narrow pathway. Soon this brings you to the village green. Cross over via a path in front of you to Church Lane opposite. There is a seat and bus shelter on the corner here.

As you walk down Church Lane you will have a good view of St John the Baptist church and to the right a lodge at the entrance to the Hall drive. Follow the lane as it bears left passing a footpath sign on your right. Note the interesting Parsonage and Old Dalby Cottage on the left. About 200 yards past the church you will find another footpath sign, on your right. Cross the stile here into a path which may be muddy as it crosses a small stream. Go over the narrow concrete bridge and then a fence into a pasture field. Cross to a metal gate opposite. Keep to the left round this field to join a rough farm track where the hedge ends. Continue to a wooden gate at the corner of the field. There are good views of the Vale of Belvoir to the left.

If the gate is closed, climb over and turn sharp left along the track, then right uphill noting a railway line to your left. There are good views of Old Dalby to your right, also a deep valley containing Old Dalby Wood. Carry on and you may see the occasional vehicle ahead plus a house which together mark the line of the Six Hills to Eastwell road.

16

At this road turn right for 250 yards until you reach the sign 'Footpath to Old Dalby' on your right leading into Old Dalby Wood. Go over the stile to the left of a wooden gate into a wide, rough stone, woodland track. Proceed downhill for some way until you reach three footpath signs on trees to your right which indicate that you must turn into a minor path here.

Soon you cross a narrow concrete bridge over a small stream and at the edge of the wood cross a stile to the right of a small gate and over another concrete bridge, uphill straight ahead to a gate at the far side in a strip of woodland known as Fishponds Wood. The gate has 'Footpath' painted on it.

Follow the woodland path downhill for 50 yards to a notice 'Beware of the Bull'. I think and believe that this is a deterrent only! Cross the stile into the field and go straight ahead aiming to the right of the Hall. Walk towards a clump of trees which mark the churchyard. You can now see the churchyard wall. Go over to the wall and follow it to reach a gate and step stile in the far corner. Cross into Church Lane. Turn left past the church for the village green. Cross it to return to the Crown via the narrow path along which you began the walk.

③ Walton-on-the-Wolds
The Anchor Inn

Walton is about as far inland as you can get so why are you invited by the convivial hosts to 'Drop anchor at the Anchor'? The nautical connection is apparently to commemorate Hobart Pasha who was born in the local rectory in 1822 and was an admiral not only in the British navy but also in the Turkish navy. Inside the spacious lounge there are many interesting curios, including an anchor as well as stone jars and pewter mugs, saddles and brasses.

This freehouse is very busy both at lunchtimes and in the evenings, especially at weekends, not only due to its fine reputation, but also because of its convenient position within easy reach of Loughborough, Melton, Nottingham and Leicester. Marston's Pedigree, Marston's Burton Bitter, Timothy Taylor Landlord Bitter, plus a premium strength guest bitter and Scrumpy Jack Old Hazy cask conditioned cider are on offer on weekdays between 12 noon-2.30 pm and

7 pm-11 pm, Sundays 12 noon-3 pm, 7 pm-10.30 pm. At the front of the pub there is a patio where the village scene can be observed whilst you enjoy your drink. Well-behaved dogs are welcome outside, and there is a garden area for families.

Undoubtedly the outstanding features of this excellent pub are the high quality food and the versatility of the menu. There are many specialities, all home-made, including the award-winning steak and kidney pie cooked in Guinness, the special lasagne and home-cooked ham, followed by a wonderful variety of sweets. All this is well supported by a choice wine list. Food is served from 12 noon-2 pm weekdays and on Sundays. A full menu is available at these times as well as in the evenings (not Sundays or Mondays) from 7 pm-10 pm. The traditional Sunday lunch is from 12 noon-2 pm. Do not miss this excellent pub.

Telephone: Wymeswold (01509) 880018.

How to get there: This is a very accessible village only 3 miles from Loughborough and 2 miles from Barrow upon Soar. From Loughborough go easterly on the A60 then follow the B676, B675 to Walton. From Barrow take the B675 and turn right for Walton-on-the-Wolds. As its name suggests the village is situated on the edge of the Leicestershire Wolds only a short distance away from the valley of the river Soar.

Parking: There is a large car park at the rear of the Anchor Inn.

Length of the walk: 3 miles. Maps: OS Landranger series 129, Pathfinder SK 41/51 (GR 593198).

Despite the hustle and bustle on the roads round and about as commuters rush to work or home each day in this busy part of the East Midlands, there is, thankfully, a peace and tranquillity about Walton. It has the ingredients of a typically English village with church, rectory, pub, thatched cottages in pleasant harmony located round a bend and with gentle undulating hills nearby.

The walk proceeds through the village, past the unusual church, then strikes across the fields to Fishpool Brook. Thence it follows a specially constructed footpath alongside the stream to the outskirts of Barrow. The return journey is via Tithe Farm, through the farmyard and then along the Wold top to reach Walton for a glimpse of the famous rectory where Hobart Pasha was born. During the walk there is a feeling of the spaciousness that this Wolds region conveys and in the distance a reminder of 20th century technology as Loughborough and its famous university appear on the skyline.

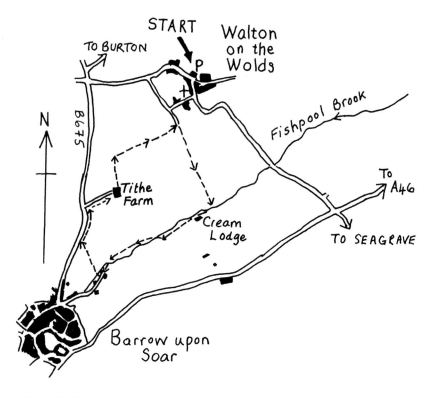

The Walk

On leaving the Anchor turn left and go uphill to New Lane. Turn right at New Lane and you will see St Mary's church on your right. The west tower is 1736 and there has been restoration in the Victorian Gothic style re-using 18th century bricks. This gives an odd appearance to the place. The chancel and vestry were rebuilt in 1856 and the nave restored in 1877. Inside, look for the carved organ seat once a choir stall in Peterborough Cathedral, according to Arthur Mee. Pevsner regards the whole thing as 'very dull' but I think you will have a different view, especially when you see the noble cedar and rectory behind. Notice also the stump of a cross, a coffin slab on the wall and the many Swithland slate tombstones in the churchyard.

Walk to the bend in the road and at the bridlepath sign on your left turn into a wide track. This leads to a large field and you must follow the track mid-field across to a metal gate at the far side. Then follow between the hedge-line and a wire fence to a gap in the hedge ahead (next field). Cross to a small wooden gate opposite. Go over a plank bridge and turn right to follow a footpath sign, climbing a stile on the way.

The footpath now follows the river. Bear left, still along the riverside. The path is mostly very clear but you will come to a point where you must deviate from the stream a little, cross a fence (unmarked, oddly), then turn right in 20 yards to find a sign which directs you across a stile and bridge so that you are now on the opposite side of the stream. Signs now appear more regularly and you just follow the stream after bearing left over the bridge. Go through metal gates until you reach a show-jumping field. Now cross a stile onto a track leading between outbuildings which are situated in Brook Lane.

In a short distance along the lane look for a notice 'Cross Country Only' on your right and turn into a metal gate. Follow the path ahead between hedges. Cross a stream bearing right alongside a hedge. In 100 yards go left through a small wooden gate into a narrow path ahead. Then go through a metal gate to skirt the allotments. The path reaches the main road, the B675, at a bridlepath sign. Turn right and walk along the verge for ¼ mile until you reach another bridlepath sign on your right leading to Tithe Farm. Follow this track into the farmyard. Then turn left through the farmyard along the track ahead. As you walk along you see Loughborough and the University tower to your left in the distance.

At the third power-line pole turn right into a bridlepath alongside a hedge. You can now see Walton ahead. Keep straight on following the edge of the field. Pass through a small wooden gate into an arable field and keep to the left side. At the far left corner turn left to return to New Lane. Alternatively, if you cross a stile in front of you, which is waymarked with a yellow arrow, it will lead you to New Lane also, but will cut off the corner for you. You arrive back near the church. A footpath sign points past the church tower. Follow this across in front of the Rectory, the birthplace of Augustus Charles Hobart-Hampden (Hobart Pasha), and into School Lane. Go down this lane and turn left at the main road to return to the Anchor Inn.

Hoby
The Blue Bell

4

This thatched pub sits opposite the old schoolhouse in a splendid Wreake Valley village with lots to discover. Inside there is a very pleasant atmosphere in the three spacious rooms. The genuine warm and friendly welcome makes even a stranger feel at home and it is unsurprising how busy the pub gets, even though away from the beaten track, due mainly to its famous reputation.

This fine pub is an Everards house with the Old Original, Beacon and Tiger Best Bitter all well kept and supported by Strongbow Cider on draught. Drinking times are 12 noon-2.30 pm and 7 pm-11 pm Monday to Friday, 11.30 am-3 pm and 7 pm-11 pm on Saturdays, 12 noon-3 pm and 7 pm-10.30 pm on Sundays.

Home-made meals are available 12 noon-1.30 pm and 7 pm-9.30 pm on Tuesdays, Wednesdays, Thursdays, Fridays and Saturdays, plus Sunday lunch (booking preferred). There is a family room and a garden area for children. Well-behaved dogs are welcome in the garden but not inside, and you can eat your own food there with your pub drink.

Telephone: Melton Mowbray (01664) 434247.

How to get there: Hoby is about 6 miles west of Melton Mowbray. Take the turning off the A607 Leicester – Melton road to Brooksby, and in 1 mile this pleasant country lane will bring you to Hoby. The Blue Bell is idyllically situated opposite the old school and close to the church.

Parking: Excellent parking and easy access to the large pub car park where cars may be left while you walk.

Length of the walk: 3 miles. Maps: OS Landranger series 129, Pathfinder SK 61/71 (GR 670175).

The river Wreake runs from beyond Melton Mowbray to join the river Soar which then links with the mighty Trent. It is subject to flooding and in some parts, especially south of Asfordby, gravel quarrying has left large lakes. A series of most interesting and historic villages line each side of the valley, located well above flood levels. These form twin settlements, invariably opposite each other, as they stand in all their beauty on their own river terraces.

The walk is an easy journey across the floodplain of the Wreake from Hoby to Rotherby, thence via a gated road to the lost village of Brooksby, depopulated in the late 14th century due perhaps to the Black Death, then across the fields to return to Hoby. There are excellent views of the whole valley, of the fringing villages and each settlement has something of unique value to see.

The Walk

Go out of the pub and proceed straight ahead going to the left of the old school, now a Field Centre. A sign on the left indicates the path to Frisby. Turn left down this path between buildings. Follow a yellow marker post on your right which leads you down to the river. At another marker post cross a bridge and stile, going diagonally left to a marker post on the far side of the field. Look back for a good view of Hoby on its river terrace.

Here turn right to a fine bridge over the river Wreake, first negotiating double gates. Cross the bridge and go straight ahead across a pasture field to a waymarked plank bridge across a side stream. Then go to a metal gate opposite and by means of the side gates cross the railway line very carefully. Ahead you will see the greenhouses of the Rotherby Garden Nursery. Walk straight ahead with the hedge on your right. You will notice signs of ridge and furrow in this field. There are lovely views back to Hoby, especially when the sun brings out the scene.

Turn right at the corner of the field into a wide farm track leading to the village street. Now turn right again along the street, using the footpath. On the left you can pause at Rotherby Wildlife Garden, where there is a natural pond and a seat, plus picnic table, to rest

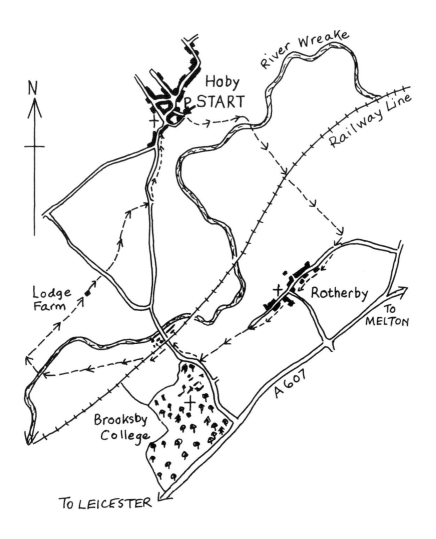

awhile. There are some fine modern conversions which fit well into the rural scene here in the village. Look left to see the quaint 'Row', now also modernised but retaining immense charm.

Carry on along the village street to follow the gated lane to Brooksby, crossing cattle grids on the way, with Brooksby spire ahead. On reaching the road turn right to the level crossing, but just before, turn left through a white gate (usually open) into the college playing fields. Here you may find portable loos and drinking water taps. As you look left towards the college you will see very finely kept grounds. The Hall and church are well worth a diversion. Admiral Lord Beatty of Jutland was once the occupier of the Hall, purchasing it in 1911.

Just before reaching the tiny cricket pavilion and scoreboard turn right to find a gate which leads across the railway line. Again, watch carefully as you cross. Go over the stile and then diagonally left towards a step-stile at the far side of the field (if you prefer, and there is a crop growing in the field, you can follow the river round via the edge of the field to your right).

From the step-stile turn right to a brick bridge over the Wreake. Make for the yellow marker post opposite, noting the abandoned river channels on your route. Turn sharp right at the post and keep to the left of the field. Hoby church is ahead of you, slightly to your left. Cross a stile and make for the left hand side of Lodge Farm ahead. Yellow marker posts again show the route clearly. Go into the farm drive and then to the lane. At the lane cross directly opposite by a stile into a field. Go across this field to the far side where you then climb a double stile with a plank bridge. Marker posts show the location.

Turn immediately left for another stile (yellow marker). Cross into a pasture field making for the church spire ahead and at the far side of this field you see a small bridge, then in front of it a stile just a few yards away. Thirty yards ahead another stile leads onto the road leading to Hoby. Turn left to walk the short distance into the village. Note the close cluster of buildings, the cruck construction of some, the Chantry and the ironstone church with its Swithland slate tombstones. A quiet stroll around this lovely and secluded village would be a worthy end to a pastoral walk.

⑤ Market Overton
The Black Bull Inn

Some of the best pubs are near churches and this one is almost opposite St Peter and St Paul's, on the edge of the village and sitting on the scarp overlooking the Vale of Catmose. Its variety of styles indicates that several smaller cottages have been attached to the original thatched building at the centre. The lovely stone matches the rest of this pretty village.

The Black Bull is a freehouse with Ruddles Best, Theakston's Black Bull Bitter, Hook Norton and Pedigree followed by Scrumpy Jack which can be drunk in the warm and hospitable lounge at the usual times. There is no beer garden, no family room, no car park (but there is plenty of space along the street). However, despite these negatives, the inn is renowned all over the area not only for the excellent real ales, but also because of the succulent bar meals at lunchtime and in the evening, as well as dining room facilities in the evenings and at Sunday lunchtime. Eating times are 12 noon-2 pm and 7 pm-10 pm every day (Sunday 9.30 pm). There is a full, fresh and varied menu at all times, except Sunday evening with the emphasis on home-made items and friendly, helpful service. The pub has been recommended in several national guides, and also offers accommodation. Well-behaved dogs are welcome.

Telephone: Thistleton (01572) 767677.

How to get there: Market Overton is about 6 miles north of Oakham and can be reached via either Ashwell and Teigh or Cottesmore. If approaching from the A1, which is only 4 miles to the east, make first for South Witham and Thistleton and then Market Overton. Rutland Railway Museum is located 2 miles south of Market Overton on the Cottesmore – Ashwell road.

Parking: The Black Bull is on the Teigh road, almost opposite the church. There is street parking in front of the pub.

Length of the walk: 3 miles. Maps: OS Landranger series 130, Pathfinder SK 81/91 Wymondham and Cottesmore (GR 887165).

Market Overton is an attractive stone-built village situated on a scarp with fine views over the Vale of Catmose below. It is only a mile or so away from Rutland's northern border. Three counties come close together here – one reason for the location of the famous championship prize-fight between Molyneaux and Cribb in 1811 watched by over 15,000 people. If the law arrived everyone could move into another county without delay! Cribb's Lodge, Thistleton Gap, a mile north of Market Overton, may mark the spot.

The remains of the Oakham – Melton Canal, which failed by the 1840s, can be seen at the foot of the scarp below the village where there is still part of the wharf building left. Ironstone quarries around the village were opened in 1906, flourishing until the 1950s, and you will see quarries, known as gullets, filled with water. Elsewhere restoration of the land can be detected by fields below road level. Once there were many mineral lines in the area. Nearby, Rutland Railway Museum has working trains as used on the ironstone lines.

The walk begins at the Black Bull and continues past the church and across the fields with lovely views over the Vale of Catmose, thence to Woodwell Head Wood and back to the village near to old gullets and a former mineral line.

The Walk

A bridlepath sign next to the church points the way down Church Lane. Follow the wide field track past Church Lane House and continue with arable fields either side. You are walking along the top of a scarp which extends throughout Northamptonshire into Rutland and then to Lincolnshire. Look below to the rich expanse of the Vale of Catmose on your left. There are views back towards the great house of Burley-on-the-Hill, not far from Oakham. Directly below you may be able to pick out a line of trees which marks the former route of the Melton – Oakham Canal.

Follow the hedge line and ash trees on your right – the path is quite obvious. Continue under the power lines bearing right. Ignore the sign 'Private' which refers to a re-colonised quarry area and not to

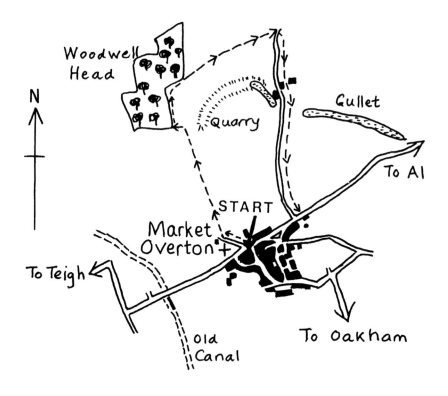

your route. Turn left at a hedge/ditch shortly after the sign, making for the corner of the woods opposite. Keeping the hedge to your left walk along the wide green track.

At the corner of the wood, Woodwell Head, you join the Berkeley Walk which has been devised by Wymondham Village Council as a path round the boundaries of their parish. You will follow part of this route. A leaflet is available, with a map showing the details of the full walk, from local libraries and from Leicestershire County Council.

Turn right to follow the edge of the wood along a rough track. At a marker post where the wood bends at right angles you also turn right still following the edge of the wood. On reaching the end of the wood, marker signs direct you straight on keeping the hedge to your left. Again this track alongside an arable field is rough. Eventually, you emerge onto a wide track leading to industrial buildings to your right. Follow the track towards these buildings. You have been walking along the boundary between Rutland and Leicestershire but now you have turned right towards Market Overton which you can see about 1 mile away.

The track turns into a concrete road and a metalled surface and you arrive at a small industrial estate. Actually, this site is a relic of the ironstone activities once carried on here and if you look closely to the left and right in the fields you will see water-filled gullets where the ore was extracted. The line of the mineral railway was to the right of the road you now follow into Market Overton but it has mostly been obliterated.

As you follow the road into the village ahead you reach the main Thistleton – Market Overton road. Turn right and cross into Bowling Green Lane on your left. This will take you through the village to give you a glimpse of the lovely buildings and gardens. At the main road in the village turn right until you reach the village green with its stocks and whipping post. Close by there are attractive stone-built cottages as well as more imposing mansions with thatched roofs and Colleyweston slates. As you proceed past the post office and general store you reach the Thistleton – Market Overton road again and by turning left you return to the Black Bull.

Before you leave the village take time to visit the church. Sited in a rectangular enclosure and associated with many Roman finds, it has been suggested that originally a Roman fort may have been located here. There has been a long continuity of settlement on this site and two large pagan cemeteries found here indicate a strong Anglo-Saxon presence. Additionally, the church contains the only Saxon remnant in Rutland, the tower arch. Fragments of pre-Conquest carved stones can be found in the outside walls of the tower and the shafts from a Saxon belfry window may now form the stone stile in the perimeter wall of the churchyard. It is said that, more recently, the sundial on the church tower was given by the great Isaac Newton who lived in the village when he visited his grandmother. All is restful serenity and a final short walk outside the churchyard downhill a little to look over the Vale of Catmose towards Teigh will give you a memory forever to cherish.

6 Exton
The Fox and Hounds

All the ingredients are here for the English village pub par excellence – village green, thatched cottages, lordly manor house in serene parkland, old schoolhouse and the shade of fine mature trees on sunny summer days. The Fox and Hounds, a 17th century former coaching inn, is an impressive feature as it stands alongside the green. Inside its elegance is reinforced by the high ceilings, hunting and military prints and general air of distinction.

There is a traditional bar where pub games such as darts, dominoes, pool and cribbage can be found, and a separate lounge features a large stone fireplace which in winter gives a glow to your thoughts. There is also a 40 seater dining room. The Fox and Hounds is well known for its traditional Sunday lunches of roast beef, pork or lamb and offers an extensive menu every day both at lunchtime and in the evening. Opening times are 11 am-3 pm and 6.30 pm-11 pm on weekdays, and on Sundays 12 noon-3 pm and 7 pm-10.30 pm. Children are welcome in eating areas, especially in the pleasant outdoor patio at the rear with its lawn and rosebeds. This is a freehouse, and Samuel Smith Old Brewery Bitter and other fine ales are kept on handpump. Accommodation is available.

Telephone: Oakham (01572) 812403.

How to get there: Exton is 2 miles north of Rutland Water and can be reached via the A606 Oakham – Stamford road. The Fox and Hounds faces the village green.

Parking: There is a car park, as well as ample parking around the village green.

Length of the walk: 4 miles. Maps: OS Landranger series 130, Pathfinder SK 81/91 (GR 925113).

Exton is one of Rutland's prettiest villages with its green and lovely thatched cottages. Around is the Exton Estate of Lord Gainsborough, now run by his son Viscount Campden. Exton Hall lies away from the main village but both the new hall and the ruins of the old hall can be seen on your walk. Also, nearby is the church with its nationally famous monuments. Although motor vehicles are banned from much of the estate, it is possible to cross it by foot as there are acknowledged rights of way. Indeed, the Viking Way enters from the north and then goes on to Rutland Water and Oakham.

The walk crosses open country with wide views and, from time to time, there is evidence to the trained eye of the old iron quarrying formerly found in this area. It proceeds to a folly known as Fort Henry set on a beautiful lakeside with the deserted medieval village of Horn just to the south. It then passes Tunneley Wood to join the Viking Way which returns to the village, and concludes with a perambulation of the villagescape.

The Walk

From the Fox and Hounds cross the green to the far corner where you reach Stamford Road. Almost opposite you there is New Field Road. Go over and walk between the bungalows until you reach a sign on a gate leading into the Exton Estate. Although private, you have access on foot because this is a right of way. Carry on along this road for about ½ mile when you bear left for another ½ mile until you reach another road crossing yours. Do not go left or right but straight on into the field opposite, where a well-marked grass lane leads to the surfaced road between Fort Henry Lake and the Lower Lake.

You will need to turn into the road on your left but before doing so take a close look at the lovely scene of Fort Henry and its lakes. Then return to follow the road mentioned. Carry on for 1 mile and eventually you pass Tunneley Wood on your left. When you come to

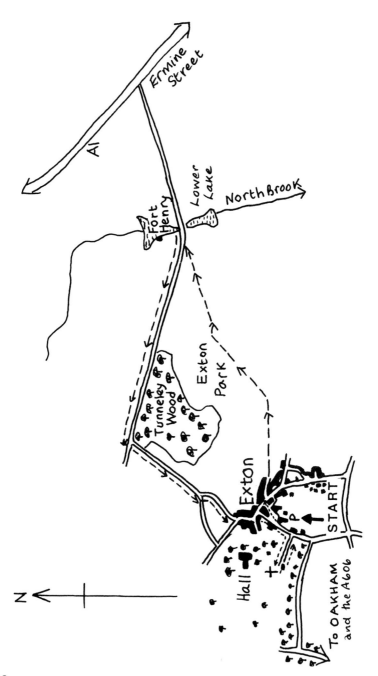

the end of the woodland turn sharp left to join the Viking Way. This goes into Exton, ¾ mile to the south, passing the cemetery on the way. Remember to take the left fork which you reach just before the cemetery.

You come to a farmyard belonging to the Exton Estate. Turn left into it via a cattle grid and side gate – there are signs here. Then follow the farm road for a short distance as it bears right into the village. Note Pudding Bag Lane on your right at the bend. Once this was the road to Cottesmore but when the new hall was built in the 1840s it had to be diverted.

Bear left with a pillared monument on your left (for the village pump) and the old Catholic school (1874-1965) on your right. You are now going down the High Street with its charming thatched cottages used as a scene in the film 'Little Lord Fauntleroy'. Carry on to pass the village hall on your right and, nearby, the Old School House, once the girls' school before 1846 then the mixed Church of England school from 1871 to 1967. Some say that the original Fox and Hounds was located in this building before it was turned to educational uses. The village green is to your left.

Walk on for about 300 yards until you see a sign 'Parish Church' on your left. This points to a lane which you must follow to reach the church. Note on your left the irregularities in the field that indicate part of the old village. To your right you will see the ruins of the old hall, burnt down in 1810, with the original landscaped gardens around it. Further across you will see the new hall, but the best view of this is from behind the churchyard.

Shortly, you reach St Peter and St Paul's, described in 1813 as 'the handsomest church in the country', but in 1843 the 14th century spire was struck by lightning and destroyed for 'several yards downwards.' Fire ensued which caused immense devastation. In 1852-53, J.L. Pearson was commissioned to restore the whole church which was largely rebuilt. Though still imposing in its solitary splendour, it is the treasures inside which draw most visitors. 'There are no churches in Rutland, and few in England, in which English sculpture from the 16th to the 18th centuries can be studied so profitably and enjoyed as much as at Exton', wrote Nicholas Pevsner. Opposite the church is Yew Tree House, a late 18th century building which was a farmhouse later, then sub-divided into almshouses.

Return down the lane to the main road. Turn left, noting just opposite you Church Farm House with a chimney dated 1684. Follow the road back to the green, turning right for the Fox and Hounds.

Somerby
The Old Brewery Inn

There is plenty of character and atmosphere in this four centuries old inn situated in the High Street. In Winter, the blazing fire enhances the cosy and spacious interior. Hankering for a taste of beer as it was in the good old days? This is the place for you as it is associated with two independent breweries. The Parish Brewery, producing on the spot the finest beers made from top quality malts and hops where the chief brewer, Barrie (Baz) Parish, makes a variety of beers including Baz's Bonce Blower, the strongest traditionally brewed ale on handpump in England, and the John O'Gaunt Brewing Co. which has recently taken on the running of the pub. This brewery produces four award winning ales including Robin a Tiptoe, Cropped Oak and Coat O'Red. All of these brews relate to local legends which the staff at the pub are only too happy to inform you of.

Visits to the Brewery can be arranged to include beer, wine and soft drinks and a buffet. The function room, once the old stables and coach house, still retains the old beams despite modernisation. The courtyard provides an excellent additional area during the summer months. There is a beer garden where you can consume your own food with the drinks you have purchased and where children can enjoy the play facilities. Well-behaved dogs are also welcome. Three rooms are available for overnight accommodation, if you can't tear yourself away.

The Old Brewery Inn has a good reputation for delicious food at reasonable prices, from filled jacket potatoes and giant Yorkshire puddings, variously filled, Somerby sausages, steaks and a huge mixed grill. Sample a ploughman's with the local Stilton cheese. There are always daily specials on offer and food is available from 12 noon every day (except Mondays) until 1.45 pm (Sunday 2 pm) and 6.45 pm until 9.45 pm (Sunday 7 pm to 9.30 pm). Drinking times: weekdays 11.30 am-2.30 pm and 6 pm-11 pm, open all day Saturdays and Sundays.

Telephone: Melton Mowbray (01664) 454866.

How to get there: Somerby is about 5 miles west of Oakham and lies off the main roads but can be reached via Cold Overton (from the A606), Great Dalby (on the B6047), or Knossington. The Old Brewery Inn is easy to find as it is in the long High Street.

Parking: There is excellent parking behind the pub which also has an overflow car park, and there will be no problem with leaving your car while you walk.

Length of the walk: 4 miles. Maps: OS Landranger series 129 and 141, Pathfinder SK 60/70 and SK 61/71 (GR 780105).

Somerby is a fine large village of brown stone buildings with some of Leicestershire's red brick too. The main street is long and has several right-angled bends in it. There are some interesting side lanes worth exploring. Since Somerby is situated in High Leicestershire it follows that you will have excellent all round views. The church is visible from many points and, besides the many other absorbing features, there is a memorial window to Fred Burnaby (1842-85). His father was the vicar and their home was Somerby Hall, now demolished. Frederick Gustavus was an English cavalry officer and intrepid traveller who followed Gordon to the Sudan, attempted to reach Central Asia, commanded a Turkish brigade in the war with Russia and flew across the Channel. He died fighting the Arabs at Abu Klea. His book 'The Ride to Khiva' was a popular Victorian travel volume.

The walk covers undulating countryside south of the village with some gated roads and some field walking. The views are always excellent and if you wish you can call in at the tiny village of Owston en route.

The Walk

Turn left out of the Old Brewery Inn car park then left again into the main street. Continue until the road takes a sharp right bend. You go into a lane to the left next to The Grove. An avenue of trees leads to

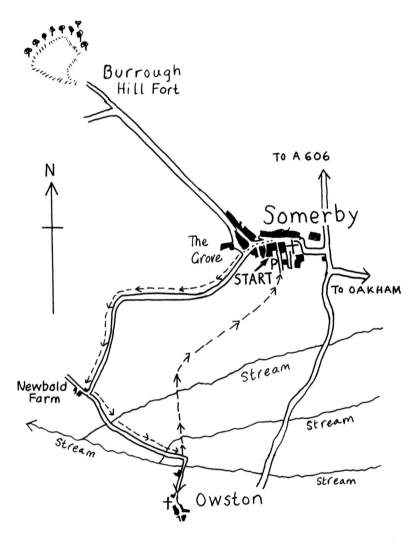

Somerby Riding School. Follow the lane as it bears left. Ignore the bridlepath sign which you pass. There are excellent views of Burrough on the Hill village to your right and, in the distance, towards the tiny village of Owston.

Soon you reach Newbold Farm where you turn left through a metal gate into the field road leading to Owston. This delightful lane crosses a small stream and then you pass through a metal gate. Around is much ridge and furrow showing that in medieval times this was cultivated land. Eventually you arrive at a signpost on your left indicating 'Leicestershire Round Bridleway to Somerby 1½ miles'. There may also be an additional sign warning of a waymarked deviation. Before you follow this path you may wish to go into Owston village which is only just round the corner. There are some charming cottages, lovely gardens, the old manor house and the remains of Owston Priory, and the church.

Turn left into the path going round the edge of a field, which may be a little rough, until you reach and cross a bridge over a stream. There is an arrow marker here. Carry on to the right hand side of the next field. At the far corner turn left to follow the field boundary to a yellow marker post. There are good views back towards Owston and the spire of Tilton church is visible in the distance to the south west.

Cross a bridge at a marker post and go straight ahead to the left of a hedge, eventually going downhill into a small valley. An arrow points through a gate into an arable field. Go round the edge of the field to the left. After 100 yards cross a side valley via an open wooden gate. Turn right to a metal gate at the corner of the field. An arrow directs you across the field to a wooden gate. Carry on alongside the hedge and power lines. At the far corner of the field go through a small wooden gate (arrow) and follow the hedgerow uphill with power lines ahead. Somerby church and village are now in sight. Go through a metal gate (arrow) and keep to the hedge on your left. Aim for a metal gate at the far side. This leads to a green lane into the village which brings you to Manor Lane. Turn right to return to the Old Brewery Inn.

You could follow your walk with a visit to Burrough Hill, 1 mile north of Somerby. At over 600 ft it is one of the county's high points. The ramparts of the Iron Age fort are clearly visible and information boards explain the layout. There is a good car park and a toposcope at the site.

⑧ Langham
The Noel Arms

This delightful old pub is charmingly situated in a narrow lane leading to the centre of one of Rutland's most dignified villages. Only 100 yards away is the hurly-burly of the busy Oakham – Melton road, but once you are in the Noel Arms you have a pleasantly settled and comfortable atmosphere in this 17th century building. There is a large lounge with a central fireplace and a restaurant. In winter a glowing fire gives the whole place a cheerful and welcoming aspect. A wide range of beers is available from Wolverhampton & Dudley Breweries, better known as Banks's, and you will find a very good variety of home-made food from the menu or specials board. The pub has an excellent reputation in the local area.

Food is available on weekdays from 11.30 am-2.30 pm and from 6.30 pm-10 pm; Sunday from 12 noon-3 pm and 7 pm-9.30 pm. En suite accommodation for large or small parties is also provided.

Telephone: Oakham (01572) 722931.

How to get there: Langham is 1½ miles north of Oakham on the A606 to Melton Mowbray. The Noel Arms is in Bridge Street, just off the A606.

Parking: A sign indicates the Noel Arms where you will find a car park. Please do not park in the narrow street outside.

Length of the walk: 4¾ miles. Maps: OS Landranger series 130, Pathfinder Wymondham and Cottesmore SK 81/91 (GR 842109).

Langham is one of Rutland's most attractive and interesting villages. It is the home of the famous Ruddles Ales and you see the brewery at the end of the walk. The village is believed to have been the birthplace of Simon de Langham, Abbot of Westminster Abbey, Archbishop of Canterbury (1366-68) and Chancellor of England. Certainly the impressive church of St Peter and St Paul with its central location, majestic spire and splendid south side reinforces the impression of religious significance.

The walk is north of Langham, in the direction of Whissendine and may follow the line of the original road between the villages. As it reaches a 450 ft ridge it turns eastwards along the parish boundaries giving good views south over the Vale of Catmose. Once across the Ashwell road, the walk turns south east, then due south to Langham Lodge with views to Burley-on-the-Hill on its scarp to your left. You enter the village and pass the brewery and church on your way back to the Noel Arms.

The Walk

From the Noel Arms, turn left into Bridge Street. Carry on until you reach Well Street and then turn right. In a short distance you turn left into Orchard Road. Go to the end and turn right into Manor Lane. Look for the sign 'Public Footpath to Whissendine 1½'. Cross the stile into a field and keep to the hedge on your left. Follow the corner round for 20 yards to a gap in the hedge on your left. Go through into the next field and continue along the hedge to your left until you reach a yellow marker post. Follow the direction of the arrow across the corner of the field and over a bridge in a clump of trees opposite.

Once across the bridge turn sharp right reaching a wooden footpath sign at the corner of the field. Turn left along the hedge. At the corner of the field which you now reach, look for a small plank bridge and marker post. Cross the bridge and follow the green track ahead uphill. At the top of the slope the track comes to a double stile. Before crossing look back for a fine view over the Vale of Catmose with Langham church and to its left Oakham church beyond. To your far left is a scarp with Burley on its crest. Tornado aircraft based at Cottesmore may be flying overhead. Once over the stiles there is a

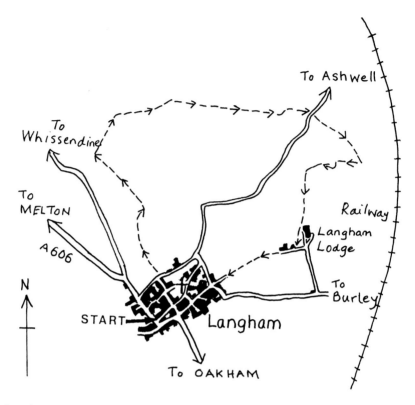

lovely view to Whissendine. Note the old windmill and far right the church tower, some distance from the main part of the village.

Turn sharp right to follow a green track. In the distance to your left you may be able to see the BBC TV transmitter at Waltham-on-the-Wolds. Carry on slightly uphill through an open metal gate as the track continues into the next field. You reach a divide in the track near a large ash tree. The left track goes to Whissendine but you keep straight ahead following the tree line to your right. There are good views to the right across to All Saints, Oakham. At the corner of the field proceed straight on through a gap leading to a path enclosed by hedges on both sides. Eventually your path emerges into a large arable field. Carry straight on alongside the hedge on your left. As you are on a ridge you have excellent views left to Ashwell and right to Oakham. The path passes a large ash tree and pond on your right.

About 100 yards further on you pass through an open wooden gate into a narrow woodland path. Bear left, still in woodland, then right to reach the Ashwell–Langham road. You have been following a bridleway along the Langham parish boundary for the last 1½ miles.

40

When you emerge onto the country lane turn right to the bridleway sign 20 yards away. Follow this path alongside a coniferous plantation. Continue between hedge and field fence and, as the path narrows, its course is still clear in front of you. Bear right near two large ash trees. At a metal gate to your right cross a stile into a large field. Follow the hedge line on your right to the far corner of the field. At the corner turn sharp left alongside a stunted hedge for 50 yards. Continue along a wide grassy track as it turns at right angles beside a hedge which bears left round the field. In ¼ mile the grassy track meets a farm track to Langham Lodge. Turn sharp left along this towards the farm buildings.

On nearing the farm cross the bridge over the stream. In about 5 yards look for an overgrown path between trees to your right. Go through for a short distance to a stile on the far side of the trees. Cross the stile into a pasture field and bear diagonally left to double power poles and sheds at the far corner. Aim for the stile which is about 40 yards to the left of the shed, under a horse chestnut tree, in the corner of the field. Cross the stile onto a concrete drive. Turn right and walk between hedges on the drive past a house. Soon the drive degenerates into a track with battery hen sheds on your right and then narrows into a pleasant single path between trees. Follow this for almost ½ mile to emerge on a surfaced lane with the village sewage works to your right. Go on a short distance to reach the main road.

To return to the Noel Arms go straight ahead following the sign for Melton Mowbray. Opposite Ruddles Brewery turn right. At Church Street turn left past the post office and shop. Follow the street back to the Noel Arms.

⑨ Empingham
The White Horse

This stone built inn set in the quiet village of Empingham in the heart of Rutland's beautiful countryside is within easy reach of Rutland Water, England's largest man-made lake. Originally it was used as the 17th century court house and opposite is the Audit Hall where tenants of Lord Ancaster of Normanton Hall paid their dues. The White Horse is situated at the corner of the village street and the busy Stamford – Oakham road (A606) and by night or day it is most eye-catching and tempting to the passer-by.

The friendly, well-stocked bar with its large cowled fireplace and beamed ceiling offers John Smith's, Directors and Ruddles ales as well as a variety of high quality bar snacks, such as home-made soup, seafood dishes, steaks, main courses, vegetarian, and Auntie June's sweets. In the restaurant there is a choice of wines and excellent food, with Rutland Trout and Rutland Platter being specialities. There is no family room but a garden for children and a beer garden are very popular. Food is available all day, including afternoon teas from 3.15 pm to 5.45 pm.

Dogs are not welcome in the public parts of the inn but would be able to accompany you whilst you drink at the tables outside. The

White Horse is a Courage house and it is open for drinking on Monday-Saturday 11 am-11 pm, and on Sunday 11 am to 10.30 pm. Accommodation is available and includes a honeymoon suite with a four poster bed.

Telephone: Stamford (01780) 460221.

How to get there: From either Stamford or Oakham follow the A606, and Empingham is about halfway between the towns. You can't miss the White Horse as you turn into the village where it lies facing the main road.

Parking: There is parking for over 50 cars behind the White Horse for patrons and the wide Main Street of the village will easily provide additional safe parking.

Length of the walk: 3 miles. Maps: OS Landranger series 141, Pathfinder Rutland Water SK 80/90 (GR 948086).

This easy walk takes you below the great earth dam holding back Rutland Water, past the pumping station which fills the reservoir from the rivers Welland and Nene to the south. You then walk up the green slopes of the dam to one end and have a bracing stretch along the crest of the dam to the far side. This gives wonderful views back to Empingham and also across most of this large reservoir. If you have time there is a short extension to see the church in the water at Normanton and then you return via Bunker's Hill into the village to see the remarkable church and Prebendary House as you stroll through this imposing estate village back to the White Horse.

The Walk

Cross the busy A606 with great care and go into Nook Lane opposite the pub. This charming and quiet lane has some lovely thatched cottages. When you reach the signpost at the end of the lane it signals Hereward Way, Rutland Water ¾ mile. Cross the stile into a pasture field and proceed diagonally towards the corner of a house on the left. A notice requires dogs to be on a lead as there are sheep, cattle and horses in these fields. Ahead you will see a very straight skyline. This is the crest of the dam, but it is so well concealed that you would never know.

A clear field path marks your route across the field to a stile which leads into another pasture field. Before you cross, look back at the site of Empingham with its distinctive church spire. Don't be afraid of the horses in the field. After crossing the stile turn sharp right to follow a wire fence. This leads to another stile, then into woodland via a plank over a small stream. Did you see the moated site and the pumping station?

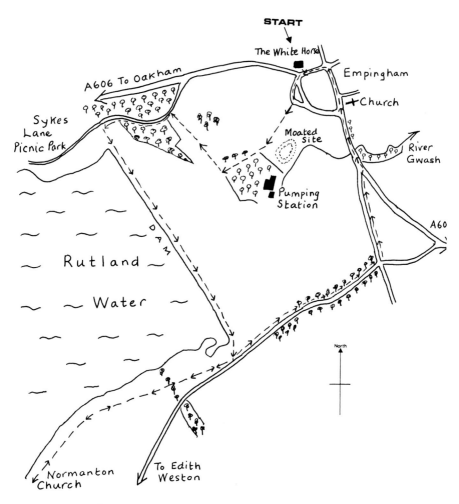

Your path now follows the edge of the woodland with a wire fence on your left. Beware some thorn bushes and brambles hereabouts. After about 5 minutes you arrive at a wooden stile. The dam crest is even clearer now and you will see cyclists and walkers along the top of it. Cross the stile and turn right across the pasture field to a metal gate at the far side. Go through the gate onto Syke's Lane. Turn left and follow this lane until you reach the dam on your left. A gate/stile marks your starting point to cross the dam. If you wish you can go down to visit the Tourist Office at the picnic park. Otherwise, climb the stile to walk the dam crest path which is a permissive route provided by Anglian Water.

44

The dam is ¾ mile long and as you walk along it there are fine views on the left to Empingham and the pumping station whilst to the right you may notice all sorts of activities such as sailing, fishing, and the *Rutland Belle* ferrying people across from Whitwell Creek to Normanton church, as well as the spire of Edith Weston church and the Hambleton Peninsula.

When you reach the far side you see the draw off tower which, if necessary, can reduce the water level in the reservoir. Here you reach a metal swing gate onto the main road. Look back at the dam and its stone facing before you move off. If you wish, you can now make a short diversion of 1 mile along the south shore of the reservoir to visit Normanton church which was saved from the flood in the 1970s largely by voluntary efforts. Close by is the excellent Normanton Park Hotel for coffee, etc. This was once the stable block and clock tower of Lord Ancaster's mansion, now demolished. If you take this diversion you return the same way to the metal swing gate.

From the gate, turn left and follow the main road keeping on the wide verge on the left hand side. In ½ mile you reach the lane signposted to Empingham. Turn left at the sign into the lane known as Bunker's Hill from where you will see Empingham in front of you. Shortly, you reach the A606. Cross very carefully to the far side and walk into Empingham crossing the bridge over the river Gwash which has now re-emerged from Rutland Water. As you look to the left you can see the even crest of the dam but no sign of the reservoir itself. The landscaping has been done so well it is hidden.

Proceed into the village bearing right into Church Street. Here you find a village store and an antique shop. Notice the gates to the prebendal manor which you can see better from the churchyard. Certainly go into St Peter's which you can approach from Crockett Lane. There are many fine buildings and outbuildings as you walk up the street and some modern infilling has been done most successfully.

When you reach the top of the street you are in Main Street and you bear left at the signpost (but have a final view back down Church Street – it is one of the most outstanding features of Rutland's villagescape). In a few minutes you will be back at the White Horse, but don't forget to notice the two working farms nearby, as well as fine stone estate houses with the family crest on them.

⑩ Belmesthorpe
The Blue Bell

This charming olde worlde pub is attractively situated downhill from the centre of the tiny village, nearly on the watermeadows of the river Gwash, but sensibly on the terrace above flood levels. There is no family room or non-smoking area, but outside is a garden with swings and fenced patio, very suitable for children.

Food is available between 12 noon-2 pm every lunchtime and every evening (except Sunday) from 7 pm-9.30 pm. A good range of home-cooked food is available. Excellent value bar meals, comfortable surroundings and a lively atmosphere. This freehouse has well-kept real ales including Bass and occasional guest ales, with Ruddles County making an appearance. The draught cider is Strongbow. Drinking times are 12 noon-2.30 pm and 6 pm-11 pm weekdays, all day Saturday and Sunday.

Well-behaved dogs are welcome and they would certainly enjoy the field walk across to Tolethorpe Hall and back. Don't forget to look for the famous Belmesthorpe Dovecote before you leave the area.

Telephone: Stamford (01780) 63859.

46

How to get there: Belmesthorpe is near the larger village of Ryhall and both are about 2 miles north of Stamford via the A6121. If approaching from the A1, make for Great Casterton then Little Casterton and the village is only 1 mile further on. The Blue Bell is on the Belmesthorpe – Ryhall road.

Parking: There is a spacious car park at the rear of the Blue Bell, and you are welcome to leave your car there while you go on your walk.

Length of the walk: 4 miles. Maps: OS Landranger series 130, Pathfinder TF 01/11 Bourne (South) and Ryhall, and TF 00/10 Stamford and Peterborough (NW) (GR 043102).

This pleasant walk, mainly alongside the lovely river Gwash, is at the far eastern extremity of the county. Indeed, by some it is known as forgotten Rutland. Since it is so close to Stamford in Lincolnshire, people gravitate in that direction more than towards Leicester.

The river Gwash begins its course in High Leicestershire then it is interrupted by Rutland Water, being subsequently released to flow towards the river Welland. Before reaching that river it takes a pronounced right-angled bend at Ryhall. In fact, Ryhall is situated in a very large river meander and Belmesthorpe is opposite only ½ mile away.

The walk begins in the river meadows below Belmesthorpe then across to Ryhall which, despite much modern development, has a fine old village centre with the outstanding St John the Evangelist church dominating the scene for miles around. Next, the walk makes it way across the fields to join the wooded valley of the Gwash at Tolethorpe. Nearby is Tolethorpe Hall, the home of the Rutland Shakespeare Company. Eventually you pass Tolethorpe Mill, then on to the cricket ground with the tiny All Saints church at Little Casterton right alongside the river with the beautiful Chantry House and Rectory Cottage close by. The return journey is via country lanes and so your pleasant two hour walk has shown you three of Rutland's attractive stone-built villages and the tranquil river Gwash.

The Walk

From the Blue Bell turn left downhill to the river. There is a lovely view to your left here. At a footbridge turn left to cross and go through a metal gate. Turn right to follow the stream but bear left a little to a stile into the next field. You see Ryhall church ahead. Aim for the telegraph pole in front and then walk towards a metal gate at a children's play area. Carry on ahead to a gravel pathway to the right of a primary school. This leads to a lane joining the village street. Cross the street into Balk Lane (spelt Baulke Lane at the other end) and proceed down it until you reach the main road (A6121). Look carefully and when it is safe to cross go to the metal gate opposite. This leads

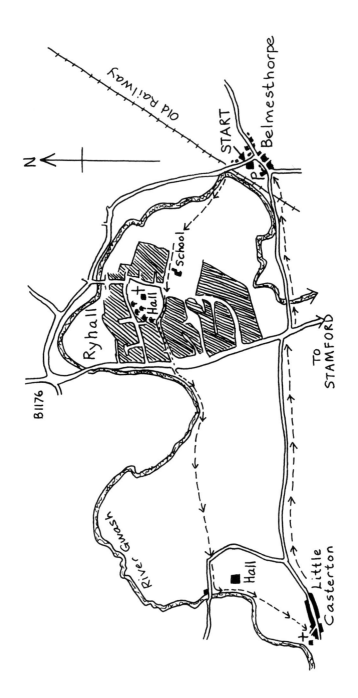

alongside the river where there is a well-defined track. Follow this for about 400 yards until the river makes a major bend away from you. Here you must turn left off the track going between two large fields uphill towards the skyline. Usually the farmer will have left a grass track between the fields to mark the way.

At the far side of the field turn left alongside the hedge for 20 yards to a fence at a gap in the hedge. Climb over and cross a small paddock to a footpath sign in the right corner. Cross a rickety fence at the sign into a lane and go down the lane to Tolethorpe Cottage, which is on your right.

At Tolethorpe Cottage turn left at the sign 'Footpath to Little Casterton ½', pondering for a while at the bridge just before you stride into the pathway. Cross the stile to the left of a metal bridge into a grassy track at the riverside. Go through a side gate as you reach an old building which is, in fact, Tolethorpe Mill. Keep to the left of a wire fence. In 20 yards you pass through a wooden swing gate to the left of the building. Remember to replace the fastenings on the gates. The path now emerges into a woodland walk alongside the river.

As you walk along you can see the back of the stage at Tolethorpe Hall. Robert Browne, so-called 'Father of Religious Non-Conformity', was born here about 1550. He pioneered congregationalism and was repeatedly imprisoned for preaching without a licence. His followers were known as Brownists and so argumentative was he that he became known as 'Troublechurch' Brown. He died in Northampton gaol in 1633. The Burton family lived at Tolethorpe for eight generations, selling the property to the Brownes in 1503.

Pass through another swing gate into a pasture field and continue between wire fences ahead. Look back for a view of the hall. When Little Casterton comes into view, where the path divides, bear right towards the church. Go through a wooden gate into the cricket field then across to a stile leading into the churchyard. You can collect the key from nearby cottages if you wish to look inside this mainly 13th century church.

Leave the church by way of the fine gravel drive. As you emerge onto the lane look right at the very attractive scene with Chantry House and Rectory Cottage. Then go down the lane to the main village road. Turn left to walk through Little Casterton. Carry on along the Ryhall road passing the main entrance to Tolethorpe Hall on your left. Keep to the right along this road and where possible on the verge. For 1 mile you have excellent views on each side to Ryhall and to Stamford. When you reach the busy main road between Bourne and Stamford, cross very carefully into the signposted lane to Belmesthorpe. This takes you back to the river and by turning left in the village at Shepherd's Walk you arrive back at the Blue Bell.

11 Barrowden
The Exeter Arms

The name Exeter Arms is found frequently in this area and it is due to the wide influence and land ownership of the Marquis of Exeter whose family have been based at Burghley House, Stamford, for centuries. In an idyllic setting opposite the village green and duck pond, after the true fashion of Olde England, this 17th century coaching inn was previously a dairy and parcel post. There is only one barn left, which now houses the Blencowe Brewing Company, and a blacksmith's shop. In the past the licensee used to keep livestock in the field next to the pub. About seven years ago the interior was substantially altered and now consists solely of a small bar with a larger room for snacks and meals.

You can savour the village scene from the patio and may even consume your own food there as long as drinks have been purchased. This freehouse stocks its own beers alongside regularly changing guest beers; plus three other regularly changing guest real ales and a cask-conditioned cider during the summer months. Drinking times are: weekdays 12 noon-2.30 pm and 6 pm-11 pm, Sundays 12 noon-2.30 pm and 7 pm-10.30 pm (closed Monday lunchtime).

Excellent food is available, usually between 12 noon-2 pm and 7 pm-9 pm every day except all day Monday and Sunday evening. The freshly cooked menu changes daily to suit seasonal availability and a traditional roast is served at Sunday lunchtime. Children's portions are available at all times. Well-behaved dogs are welcomed. There are three en suite letting rooms available.

Telephone: Morcott (01572) 747247.

How to get there: Barrowden is about ½ mile from the A47, 16 miles west of Peterborough and 7 miles south west of Stamford. It lies on the boundary between Rutland and Northamptonshire, marked by the river Welland, and you can also approach from the A43, turning off at Wakerley Woods.

Parking: The car park is at the rear and street parking (with discretion) is also possible.

Length of the walk: 2½ miles. Maps: OS Landranger series 141, Pathfinder SK 80/90 Rutland Water and SP 89/99 Corby (North) and Uppingham (GR 947001).

This easy and most pleasant walk explores the lovely watermeadows of the river Welland. It trespasses into Northamptonshire a little to visit Wakerley which is close to both the beautiful Fineshade Woods and Wakerley Great Wood with their forest trails and picnic sites. The return journey is past the old station house and the disused railway line which ran to Kingscliffe and Wansford, then across the meadows to Barrowden. For much of the walk you will have a fine view of the village and its church, St Peter's, with its 14th century broach spire radiant on sunny days.

Thomas Cook, 'Father of Modern Tourism', started his career in Barrowden in 1828 as an itinerant Baptist missionary, and he married in St Peter's in 1833, before moving to Market Harborough and arranging the world's first package tour, from Leicester to Loughborough, in 1841.

The Walk

As you leave the Exeter Arms go left past the great horse chestnut tree, the seat and the shelter to the main street. Follow this until you come to Mill Lane, a no through road. Bear right down the lane and at a footpath sign continue to bear right to a metal gate. This leads you into a tree-lined track past a stagnant pool, probably the old mill pond. Skirt around the pond eventually turning right to cross a footbridge over the river Welland. Go through a wire gate into a pasture field. You are now on the floodplain of the river. Go across the field to a line of trees opposite which marks the line of a disused railway. As you walk look back for a very fine view of St Peter's and Barrowden on a river terrace, above flood levels. Beyond you will see the restored Morcott windmill on the skyline. Pass through a wooden swing gate

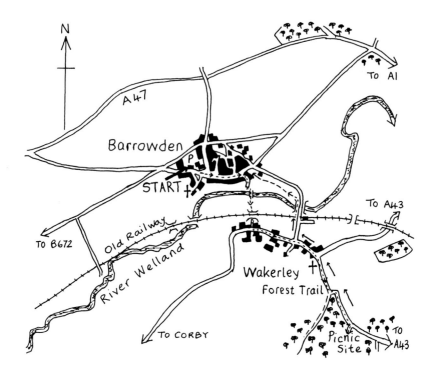

under a railway bridge and proceed uphill to a farmhouse on your left.

At the road turn left along the village street of Wakerley. There are some very fine stone houses and cottages to be seen and also several exquisite gardens. Carry on past another Exeter Arms which is on your right. This is yet another reminder of the great influence of the Cecil Family, owners of much land in Rutland, and around their home at Stamford. Indeed, they had a great mansion opposite the present Exeter Arms here which is now identified only by the terraces and irregularities in the field.

Continue to the church of St John the Baptist on the road to Fineshade. This has a very well-kept churchyard and the church itself is most impressive, being now maintained by the Redundant Churches Fund. If you care to carry on for only 500 yards you will come to the picnic site, toilets and trails in Wakerley Wood.

Return to Wakerley village noting an excellent abandoned farmyard on your right at the corner, opposite the old rectory. At the Exeter Arms turn right down the lane signposted Barrowden ½ mile. Shortly, you see on your right the former railway station. Note that the old bridge has gone and just beyond you see the sign 'Rutland'. Cross the river bridge and look both left and right at the lovely river meadows and the gently flowing stream. Then find the footpath sign pointing towards Barrowden, with the church visible in the distance. Cross the stile into the field and go diagonally right to the end of a line of trees, crossing a plank bridge on the way.

At the corner of the trees note a stile standing on its own. This must be the only stile in England without a fence or hedge. You have no need to climb over it, but simply walk round it. Now bear diagonally right following the power lines to reach a more normal stile in a hedge. Cross into a paddock. Turn left and follow the hedge and fence round the paddock. At the corner turn left to a public footpath sign and stile. After about 10 yards turn left to cross a rickety stile which leads you to Mill Lane ahead. Cross a stile into the lane.

Now make your way back to the village duck pond but instead of going straight into the Barrowden Exeter Arms go on down the lovely lane to St Peter's church passing Pepperday Cottage and Carey's House. Ponder for a while in the church and churchyard and then return for your drink. Rushes are still strewn on the day of the patronal festival at this church. Count the ducks as you pass them – from time to time they are in short supply. Not long ago they had all disappeared, most regrettably, as we have otherwise assembled here all the classic components of the English village par excellence.

⑫ Lyddington
The Old White Hart

As with so many lovely old stone buildings in English villages, this pub has its side to the main street and extends a very long way back at right angles to the street so that you go in through a drive into the car park and then enter what is really the front of the pub. Greengage and apple trees overhang the attractive garden and there are picnic tables also on the patio in front of the building.

Inside you will find a real country pub atmosphere with a small bar, a medium-sized lounge and the Hunters Restaurant (a non-smoking area) – you can choose where to eat. There is a strong emphasis on fresh, home-cooked food which matches the season. The new style menu changes every two months. There is home-made sausage and mash, fresh Grimsby haddock deep fried in crisp batter, roast of the day with fresh vegetables and all the trimmings, half a crispy duck, rack of English lamb, and much more. These are well supported by fresh vegetables, side orders and home-made puddings, plus a vegetarian menu which is always available. Light lunches are equally varied and tasty at a reasonable price. The full à la carte menu is available from 12 noon-2 pm and 7 pm-10 pm every day (not Sunday evening) and a traditional roast is served, in addition, at Sunday lunchtime.

This freehouse has Greene King IPA, Marston's Pedigree Bitter and Abbot Ale. Drinking times are 12 noon-3 pm and 6.30 pm-11 pm except Sunday evening 7 pm-10.30 pm. Since the pub is so accessible to Uppingham and Corby it soon gets busy, even on weekdays, in season. Petanque is played most evenings during the summer.

Telephone: Uppingham (01572) 821703 (bookings for the Hunters Restaurant advisable).

How to get there: Lyddington is just off the A6003 between Uppingham and Corby, Northamptonshire. It is nearer Uppingham, being only about 2 miles south east. The village is approached via pleasant country lanes and the Old White Hart is next to the village green.

Parking: There is a large, attractive, excellent car park at the pub, and you can leave your car there while you go on your walk.

Length of the walk: 4¾ miles. Maps: OS Landranger series 141, Pathfinder SP 89/99 Corby (North) and Uppingham (GR 875970).

'Long' Lyddington is one of Rutland's most beautiful and interesting villages. The Bede House (English Heritage) and the church are close together near the village green where the stump of a cross is a reminder that in medieval times the village was a market centre, vying with Uppingham. The walk follows the field path to Seaton passing close to Prestley Hill and the Barrows with lovely views of both villages. Then a country lane takes you into the Welland valley with a short pause to see Thorpe by Water. From here another pleasant country lane returns you to the southern end of the village and as you stroll back to the Old White Hart you can observe the rich ironstone buildings and lovely gardens, noting a datestone here and there.

The Walk

From the Old White Hart cross over the green to footpath signs near the swings. Do not go down Bluecoat Lane but carry straight on between a house and cottage in front of you. A sign points the way. Notice to your right the views of the church and the Bede House. You come to a stile. Cross over and then keep to the hedge on your left. You will see lots of humps and bumps in the field. Look carefully and they will appear to form a series of rectangles. These were the fishponds or stews attached to the Bishop of Lincoln's palace, now the Bede House.

Turn left through a gap in the hedge into a wide green way with the village football pitch in the field on your left. In about 100 yards cross a stile, slightly overgrown, onto a farm track which may be muddy. Turn right and cross a stile into rough pasture. Follow the hedge uphill to the far left corner where you cross another stile into a large arable field.

Again, follow the hedge through the field looking back for excellent views of Lyddington. To your right is Prestley Hill. At the corner of the field turn right for about 40 yards then go through a gap in the hedge leading to a track to Seaton, which you can see in the distance. There is a ditch to your left and you are in a very large arable field, perhaps an example of hedge-loss or prairie farming. Continue to bear right round the perimeter of the field on a wide grassy track. Bear left round a large willow tree and as you walk along you have a line of ash trees to your left.

You reach Seaton Grange Farm with a metal gate and stile to cross into a metalled farm track leading to Seaton. Note a line of poplars to your left and, in the distance, views of the Harringworth Viaduct over the Welland valley. At the main street turn right passing the village sign and lovely walls invaded by all manner of plants. Houses on the left have 1881 datestones. If you have time you could explore Seaton and look in All Hallows church. To continue your walk you need to turn right into Moles Lane and follow it down into the Welland valley. As you walk along this sunken lane remember to look back at Seaton sitting on its hill. Continue downhill bearing right along the lane until you reach the main Morcott – Caldecott road, the B672. Turn right for ½ mile and, though this road is fairly quiet, take care as there will be vehicles coming round the bends. Soon you reach the sign indicating Thorpe by Water to your left. Go into this little village which is so close to the Welland, a danger spot in time of floods.

When you are ready to proceed, return to the main road and turn left for ¼ mile until you reach a lane leading to Lyddington. Turn right into this narrow country lane and in 1 mile, with some uphill walking but great views towards Rockingham Castle and its scarp overlooking the Welland valley, you arrive back in Lyddington, and turn right to return to the inn.

Take time, if you can, to visit the Bede House, open daily from April to September (admission charge). St Andrew's church just beyond has some outstanding features including a 15th century rood screen, a little wall painting, a communion rail of 1635, acoustic jars and elegant arcades.

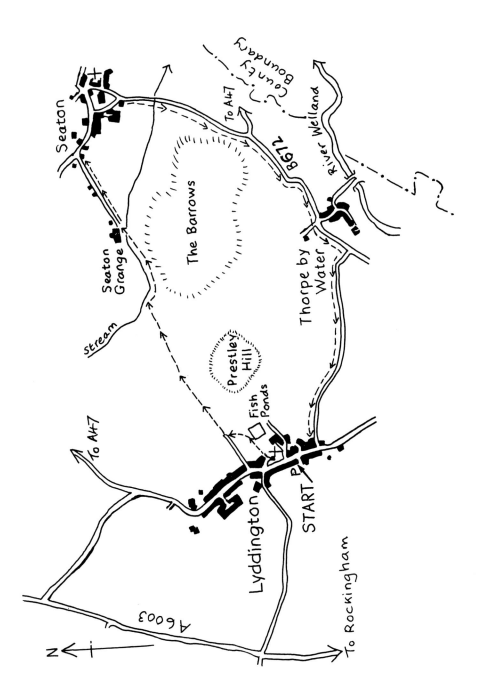

Seaton

The Barrows

Seaton Grange

stream

To A47

County Boundary

River Welland

B672

To A47

Thorpe by Water

Prestley Hill

Fish Ponds

To A47

Lyddington

START

To Rockingham

A6003

N

⓭ Bisbrooke
The Gate Inn

This pub has no pretensions to grandeur or elegance. It is an everyday local which happens to be in an outstanding position, looking out over a deeply-incised valley. In summer the lovely terraced garden, with its fine walnut tree, may be full of visitors, but in winter as you enter the bar you may be greeted with surprise by the few locals well ensconced in this freehouse, drinking their Tartan, Carlsberg, Fosters or Scrumpy Jack. Drinking times are weekdays 11 am-2 pm, 6 pm-10 pm, Sundays 12 noon-3 pm, 7 pm-10.30 pm. You can consume your own food in the garden as long as you buy your drink at the pub, and it is lovely for children, as well as good dogs.

The pub overlooks a fine valley and although it seems to be in the

58

back of beyond, in fact it is very handy for the A47 and Uppingham. Additionally, you are quite close to the Welland valley. If you like a simple, undemanding country pub, this is surely it.

Telephone: Uppingham (0572) 823453.

How to get there: Bisbrooke is close to the A47. Look for signs between Uppingham and Glaston directing you to the village which is about ½ mile to the south of the main road. If approaching from Uppingham take the Seaton road out of town and turn off for Bisbrooke in 1 mile.

Parking: The Gate Inn has a small car park but it is rather awkward getting out of it. It is better, therefore, to park sensibly in the village streets, but please take care not to obstruct entrances.

Length of the walk: 2 miles. Maps: OS Landranger series 141, Pathfinder SP 89/99 Corby (North) and Uppingham (GR 883995).

Bisbrooke lies just 1 mile east of the attractive market town of Uppingham and both share the same high ridge. Two small streams flow north and south of Bisbrooke joining a little beyond the village to reach the river Welland. The village itself has a remote feel about it and a rambling layout in which it is easy to get lost. Though much modern building is interspersed with the old, the undulating land and many good 16th, 17th and 18th century houses in lovely local brown ironstone provide an authentic character.

This is a gentle stroll towards Uppingham along the fairly flat ridge-top and back again, with excellent distant views to the Welland valley.

The Walk

At the rear of the Gate Inn look for a yellow marker at a kissing gate. Follow the path to the left of the hedge. The spire in the distance is that of Uppingham church. Bear left at the far corner of the field to a stile with a yellow arrow. Cross into the large field and go straight ahead towards the church spire in front of you. There are good views into a side valley. Can you see the old railway bridge? This is a remnant of the Uppingham link built in 1894, closed in 1964, which joined the Rugby – Stamford line (1850-1966), some 2 miles east of Bisbrooke. The Uppingham link was the last railway line to be built in Rutland.

Continue to the right of the hedge dividing two fields until you reach a well-marked wooden fence ahead. Cross into the next field keeping to a fence and hedge on your left. Views of Uppingham School's thatched cricket pavilion now appear. At the corner of the field cross the stile (arrow) into the cricket field. Go to the right of the tennis court aiming for a footpath sign in the hedge opposite. Check your watch by the pavilion clock.

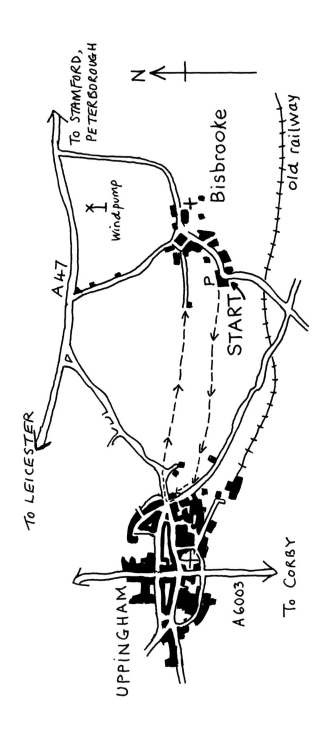

N

To STAMFORD, PETERBOROUGH

Bisbrooke

old railway

A47

Windpump

P

P

START

To LEICESTER

UPPINGHAM

To CORBY

A6003

Cross a stile onto the Uppingham – Seaton road and turn right along it. At the main road, signposted Glaston Road, turn right and keep on this side. The pavilion is now close on your right. You can see into the highly interesting High Street East, Uppingham, just before you turn. Look for the sign 'Public Footpath to Bisbrooke' 100 yards ahead. Turn right, then bear left into a wide dirt track round a farmhouse. The track continues through fields and its course is very clear. To your left you will see traffic on the former A47 some distance away. Thankfully, the bypass has made Uppingham a much quieter place.

The track narrows alongside a fence, eventually entering bushes at a yellow marker post. The path emerges and is clear ahead through rough ground. Then it widens as the village is approached. Houses and a yellow marker post are to your left as you walk down a lane known as Inhams into Bisbrooke. On reaching the village lane, known as Top Lane, turn right. Then, in 100 yards, at the main road turn right, keeping to the footpath on your left past old stone cottages, modern houses and bungalows and some farms until you reach the Gate Inn at the bend in the road.

⒕ Wing
The King's Arms

This lovely stone-built pub dates from the early 17th century and it extends at right angles to the village street. Recently it was enlarged and refurbished so that it offers excellent facilities. The old village bakehouse is opposite the main pub building and between the two is a lane leading to the car park. There are tables outside the main door and a lawn at the rear. Inside you find a real Rutland atmosphere with a winter fire, a cosy bar and lounge, plus a distinguished restaurant. People come from far and wide to eat here. There is a wide choice of home-cooked food with the emphasis on fresh produce and local dishes. Stilton figures prominently and the specials board is always a welcome sight to the visitor. Food is served from 12 noon-2 pm and 6.30 pm-9 pm on weekdays, and on Sundays from 12 noon-2 pm and 7 pm-8 pm both in the bar and restaurant.

This is a freehouse and features many popular and unusual real ales. Drinking times are 12 noon-3 pm (or longer if customers are numerous) and 6.30 pm-11 pm; Sundays from 12 noon-3 pm. In the summer months it is open all day Saturday and Sunday. There is a most busy and lively atmosphere in this well-frequented and popular pub.

En suite accommodation is available and there are special rates for walkers at certain times of the year. All rooms are non-smoking. Sorry, no pets.

This is a good base for Rutland Water and don't forget the nearby maze. Telephone: Manton (01572) 737634.

How to get there: Wing lies between Oakham and Uppingham. Take the A6003 linking both places and turn off at Preston. Wing is signposted 1½ miles from the A6003.

Parking: There is a large car park at the King's Arms and also street parking is available.

Length of the walk: 4 miles. Maps: OS Landranger series 141, Pathfinder SK 80/90 Rutland Water (GR 892029).

Wing is situated on a ridge above the river Chater. Not far away to the north, lies Rutland Water. The village must be considered logical in its layout with a Top, Bottom and Middle Street. It is famous for its Turf Maze, one of the few in England. Opposite to this the Wing Treatment Works purifies the water supplies from Rutland Water before distribution over a wide area. There are many attractive stone houses and lovely gardens, some dating from the 17th century.

The walk is over the fields, crossing a railway line and the river Chater thence northwards towards the Lyndon Nature Reserve, but before reaching that the route follows a pleasant country lane to the village of Lyndon with its impressive Hall and fine church forming a picture postcard scene. Lyndon Hall was the home of Thomas Barker, 'Father of English Meteorology', who, in the 18th century, kept records for more than 60 years. The journals of the squire are now a wonderful record of nature, the countryside and the weather 200 years ago.

The return is through quiet fields and woodland where the rest of the world seems far away and one can pause for a philosophical thought along this pastoral route.

The Walk

Go down Church Street until you reach the northern extremity of the village. Here you find a footpath sign and a metal gate. Go into the field, closing the gate behind you and make for the hedge to your right. Follow this until you reach a hunting gate and plank bridge near to a large ash tree. Cross the ditch here and turn sharp left then right, parallel with the railway line. This is the Birmingham – Peterborough line and is quite busy. Follow the broken down fence which is on your left until you reach a rail crossing point in about 100 yards. Looking back you have fine views of Wing on its ridge.

If the crossing gates are locked you will need to climb over – but this is a permissible crossing point. Take care and look in both

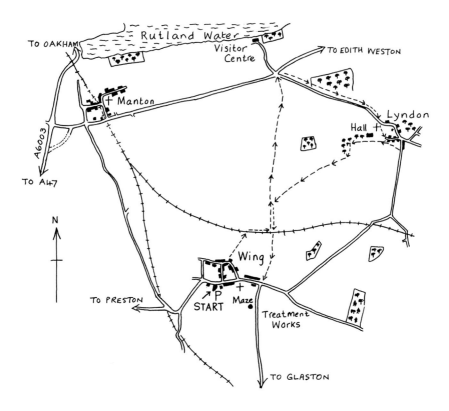

directions. Turn right along the edge of an arable field following a wire fence still keeping parallel with the railway line – you are now on the opposite side of the line. In 5 minutes or so you reach another set of crossing gates and the junction of two farm tracks. Turn left along the hedge line to follow a broad and well-defined track which is, in fact, a bridleway. Manton comes into view to the north west. Soon you cross a bridge over the river Chater. Carry on, keeping the hedge to your right as you go uphill. Pause at a gap into a field to look back at Wing and its church.

Proceed along the path straight ahead with a small wood to your right. The route is very clear. You then reach the main Manton – Edith Weston road. Opposite you see notices to the Lyndon Nature Reserve. Turn right to Lyndon which is signposted, via an avenue of oaks and ashes. Note the lovely pond on your right at a stone bridge near Lyndon Wood.

To your left you may see Lyndon Top Hall, but soon you arrive at one of Rutland's prettiest scenes. Lyndon Hall with its fine clock tower is down a drive to your right. A little further on is St Martin's church. Turn right to visit the church. At the same time look through the arch to get a glimpse of the Hall. Can you find the tombstone of William Whiston – 18th century mathematician, philosopher and divine, and father-in-law of Thomas Barker? It is propped up next to the wall. Nobody has yet found the tombstone of the 'Father of English Meteorology', who was also the brother-in-law of the famous naturalist Gilbert White of Selborne, Hampshire.

Now look for a small gate in a wall – you have to retrace your steps to find it. Go through into a secret garden and follow the walk quietly until you reach another gate. Go through this into Post Office Lane in the village. Here you see old houses and also some modern houses built in the old style using stone. At the crossroads turn right for 200 yards and look for a footpath sign on your right. Go into the field as indicated, keeping to the edge of the field bearing right. The Chater valley and Wing come into view to your left.

You soon pass in front of Lyndon Hall. Once the village street ran here but the squire altered it so that he had more privacy. Follow the edge of the wood bearing left downhill. You come to a marker post and hunting gate. The arrow points left as you proceed through the wood. Once through this small and narrow wood turn left again to follow the edge of the wood. Shortly, another marker post directs you right along a hedge. Turn left again at the next marker post, about 5 minutes away, and walk downhill to the river Chater, bearing right following the hedge line and eventually passing a poplar plantation.

At the corner of the field turn left through the plantation then bear right to cross a plank bridge and join the main farm track at the bridge over the Chater which you crossed earlier on the walk. Cross the bridge making for the railway level crossing straight ahead. Cross the line carefully via metal gates then go uphill along the bridleway to the village street. On reaching the main road turn right for the King's Arms just beyond the church. You may wish to see the Turf Maze and if so you can take a short 200 yards diversion en route to the left to do so.

⓯ **Braunston**
The Old Plough

Set in the heart of hunting country, this old coaching inn is very well placed only 2 miles away from Oakham, the former county town of Rutland. The pub presents a very welcoming face to road travellers at the bend in the busy main road.

Inside is a through bar with a beamed ceiling and brasses, with hunting prints as well as a Poacher's Survival Kit on the wall to add to the atmosphere. Reputedly the largest horseshoe in Rutland makes a fine entrance to the attractive garden where you can sit with the family for your drink, snacks or meals. Barbecues are held on special occasions, and there is a pétanque area where games are played regularly. For more sedate eating with a semi-oriental touch, there is the lovely conservatory dining room. Meals are available seven days a week from 12 noon-2 pm and 7 pm-10 pm (9.30 pm Sundays).

The Old Plough is renowned for its excellent menus. Some of the famous specials are home-made steak and kidney pie cooked in Guinness, fresh salmon with prawns wrapped in filo pastry served on a fish yoghurt sauce, fillet of sole stuffed with crabmeat and baked with a lobster and cream sauce, and, of course, 'Plough Crusty', really large home-baked granary rolls with a choice of Cheddar, Stilton, beef, ham, prawns and smoked turkey all served with a salad garnish and coleslaw. Menus change every eight weeks.

This is a freehouse where Theakston and John Smith's feature, supported by Rutland bitters from the Grainstore Brewery and Scrumpy Jack cider on draught. There is a non-smoking area. Children are welcome for meals in the Conservatory dining room and in the garden. Dogs may join you away from the food areas.

Telephone: Oakham (01572) 722714.

How to get there: Braunston is 2 miles from Oakham on the Tilton (Leicester) road. The Old Plough is on the corner if you enter the village from Oakham.

Parking: There is good parking at the Old Plough but make sure you are using the facilities. If you plan to walk first please go in to ask the landlord about parking. There is street parking in the village.

Length of the walk: 3¾ miles. Maps: OS Landranger series 141, Pathfinder SK 80/90 Rutland Water (GR 835069).

The area you are walking in was formerly the Royal Forest of Leighfield. Now, the only remnants are in the very old hedgerows and ancient woodland like Prior's Coppice. This was the frontier between Rutland and Leicestershire and you will walk along part of the boundary. There are good all-round views, especially back towards the forest village of Braunston, your starting point.

The Walk

Turn left on leaving the Old Plough down the village street to the church about 5 minutes away. All Saints is situated above the river Gwash on a slight eminence. Go into the churchyard via the main signposted pathway. You should make time to look inside the church to see the fine Norman features, 15th century wall paintings and memorials to the Cheseldyne family. As you continue along the path past the west end of the church look for the pagan fertility figure, standing grotesquely at the foot of the tower. For years, this figure was used as the threshold to the church so that everyone entering could stamp on what was thought to be the devil. Later it was rescued and placed in its present position.

Climb over the wooden fence and cross the pasture field to a metal gate opposite. At the sign, go through into the ridge and furrow field and cross to the far right hand corner. Now cross fences and a plank bridge over a tiny side stream, following the hedge line, keeping it on your right. Here you will notice a small but deep river valley to your

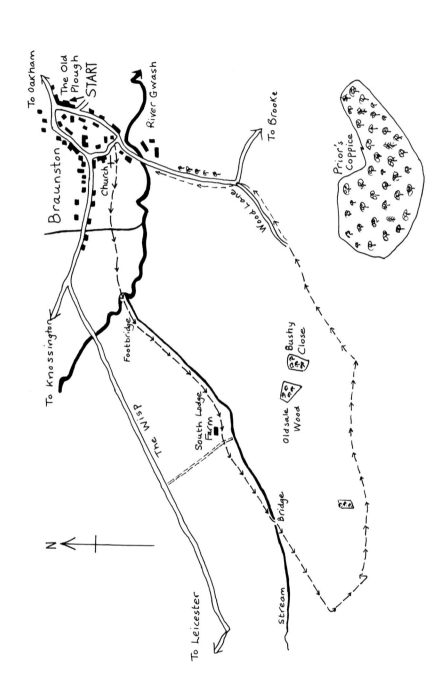

Braunston

To Oakham

The Old Plough

START

Church

River Gwash

To Brooke

Wood Lane

To Knossington

Footbridge

Prior's Coppice

Bushy Close

Old Sale Wood

South Lodge Farm

The WISP

Bridge

Stream

N

To Leicester

left which is the river Gwash.

Look for an overgrown fence and footbridge in the corner of the field. Cross it and you see a sign on the far side. Bear left towards an ash tree but before reaching it turn right along the course of a small stream. In 150 yards your path continues between two hedges with the stream still on your left. Enter an arable field via the gate and continue with the stream and hedge to your left. Go through a gate opening and carry on with the hedge and stream still to your left. When you reach the corner of the field cross a wooden fence into a pasture. Cross to a metal gate opposite. At the gate note a house to your right, South Lodge Farm. Go over or through the gate into rough ground still following the stream on your left. Cross over a farm track and continue ahead into and across a pasture field. At the far top corner of this field you will find a gap. Go through this gap into the field then bear diagonally across downhill to find a bridge and gates which take you over the stream.

Now cross the field making for a stunted ash tree at the top of the hill. Follow the hedge to the far corner of the field and under a large ash tree cross over a wooden fence into a large arable field. Look opposite to the far side of the field to find a bend in the hedgeline then cross the field to the left of this bend looking for a gap leading onto a bridlepath. If a crop is growing in the field you may have to wend your way through tractor paths to reach the far side.

Now you are on a fine, wide and grassy pathway which also marks the boundary of Rutland. You are walking on a ridge which is 600 ft high and gives excellent views. To your right you can see Robin-A-Tiptoe Hill with a flat top and Withcote Lodge. In the distance Launde Park Wood, which is part of the Launde Abbey estate, completes a lovely prospect.

Turn left to follow the bridleway until it appears to end in a cul-de-sac. Go left through an open metal gate at the 'end' of the bridleway into an arable field where you will find that the grass track continues round the field. Do not go through an inviting gap into the next field but stay where you are, following the hedgeline and keeping it on your left. Carry straight on through several fields for about ¾ mile passing through gaps in each field along a clear route. Eventually, a large patch of woodland comes into view ahead. This is Prior's Coppice. Turn left through an open wooden gate into a pasture field. Follow the track around the field to a narrow gap in the hedge on the far side. You now emerge on to a very wide grassy track between ash trees. In 200 yards this narrows, then widens a little, finally becoming a stone track and then Wood Lane. This joins the Brooke-Braunston road and you turn left for a pleasant stroll downhill into Braunston passing farm buildings and bridges over the Gwash as you see the church ahead.

16 Keyham
The Dog and Gun

This pleasant pub is tucked away in one of Leicestershire's quietest villages. The cosy lounge and bar are very inviting and often full, as many people from Leicester's suburbs can dash out quickly for a snack and a drink. This Everards pub has Tiger, Beacon, Traditional Mild, Adnams and a guest beer. Strongbow and Woodpecker cider are on draught. Drinking times: 12 noon-2.30 pm every day (Sunday 3 pm) and 7 pm-11 pm (Sunday 10.30 pm). There is a patio (in lieu of a garden) where children, adults and dogs can congregate.

Excellent and reasonably-priced bar food is available from 12 noon-2 pm every day and on Tuesday to Sunday in the evening between 7 pm and 9.30 pm, and Monday evenings 7 pm-9 pm. Specials are on offer and these show an excellent variety of choice. They are written up on a blackboard each day. There is a good wine list in support.

Incidentally, there are 10 pubs in the county called Dog and Gun and one Dog and Hedgehog.

Telephone: Hungarton (01162) 595226.

How to get there: Keyham is about 3 miles off the A47 at Houghton on the Hill. Follow the sign down a country lane via Ingarsby. Alternatively, you can reach Keyham from Leicester via Scraptoft.

Parking: There is a large car park at the Dog and Gun.

Length of the walk: 4 miles. Maps: OS Landranger series 141, Pathfinder SK 60/70 (GR 669065).

This walk takes you through the classic landscape of medieval deserted villages in the boulder clay country of eastern Leicestershire. Although the lost villages of Quenby, Baggrave and Lowesby are close by, it is the famous site at Ingarsby which is the gem and which can be seen so clearly on the ground. This is also well-known fox-hunting country as Billesdon Coplow and Botany Bay Covert are within sight. A prehistoric routeway crosses the area from Ingarsby to Covert Lane, Scraptoft, and a former railway line with many embankments and cuttings features along the walk. Boots are advisable as you will encounter mud in the field sections.

There is a strong sense of the past as you walk along and also a feeling of remoteness, and the beauty of the gently undulating terrain is a constant delight.

The Walk

On leaving the Dog and Gun turn left into Snow's Lane. Bear left down the lane ignoring the footpath sign on your right. The bridleway you soon reach goes through private property, a boarding kennels and cattery, but do not be put off by barking dogs as you are entitled to use this path. Go forward to a wooden gate opposite and follow a grass track between hedges. Pass through a side gate to the left of a white wooden gate. Then turn left across a small stream and through a white gate going uphill diagonally to a stile and plank bridge in the far corner (arrow).

Cross to the path on the other side and follow to the left. At an open metal gate turn sharp right along a hedge (do not go straight on). At the corner of the field go through two gates over the old railway. Billesdon Coplow is in the distance. Carry on along to the left of the hedge to the gate ahead. Continue straight forward into the next field, also to the left of the hedge. Pass gates to your right and go on to the metal gate ahead in the corner of the field.

Cross the field to a gate at the left corner then go ahead to a gate at the far side. Go through a rickety metal gate and turn left onto a wide grass track. In 50 yards go through a wooden gate into rough pasture. Now go diagonally across the rough pasture, as an arrow indicates, to a telegraph pole and gate beyond. Pass through this gate and ahead are the mounds of the lost village of Ingarsby. Go ahead to the motte known as Monk's Grave which is above the main village

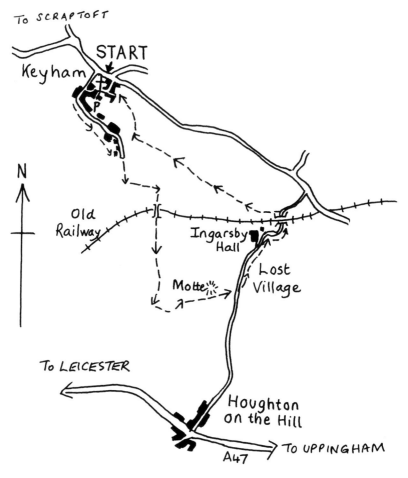

site. Pass round the mound and go downhill to a gap on a country lane. Turn left along this and go over the bridge, looking left at the old fish ponds and right to see the ridge and furrow of the old village. Leicester Abbey once owned the village but it was depopulated in 1469 when it was turned over to the more profitable sheep farming.

As you proceed along the lane you pass Ingarsby Old Hall on your left. This was probably the site of a monastic grange but some parts date from 1470. There are enlargements dating from 1579 and it was refronted in 1706. Go beyond the Hall entrance, ignoring the footpath sign here and carrying on a little further until you have passed under the old railway 'bridge'. Perhaps you can see to your right the former railway station, now nicely converted to a house? Look on your left for a footpath sign (arrow) which may be overgrown. Here, cross the stile into a field and follow the hedge on your left across the field. At the corner keep close to the stream and cross a fence to a yellow post beyond the hedge. Carry on at the edge of the stream round the field (marker post indicates). Eventually you reach a yellow post round the far corner. Turn left to cross a stile near the stream (arrow) and keep to the left hand side of the next field.

You reach a good track. Turn right to follow it uphill. In 50 yards cross a stile to the left (arrow). At the opposite side of a small paddock cross to a gate (arrow). Go over a stile and walk ahead to a white marker post. Climb a wooden fence and cross a field to an arrow on a fence post straight ahead. Go under a wire fence at an arrow post then ahead to another fence and arrow. This indicates diagonally across the field to the right of a pylon, crossing a couple of fences on the way. There is a yellow arrow to the right of the pylon.

Cross a stile and turn left diagonally towards the far corner of the field. In undergrowth there is a yellow marker post and stile. Cross, turning right along a narrow path behind some houses. Follow the path round to the left, also between buildings (arrow) with a fence on your right. The village lane is now on your left and so you can follow the Main Street back to the Dog and Gun.

There is a well-situated seat facing the church where you can pause and reflect on your walk. A red telephone box, village pump, and shining weathercock remind us of the typical English village. The charming church of All Saints is warmly brown in the sun. There are memorials to the Miles family and sad tablets to losses in the First World War. Keyham is potentially a good place to live, for it is reported that, in the past at least, 'there was an impressive longevity of the inhabitants, with people living to the great ages of 70, 80, 92 and beyond'.

⟨17⟩ Billesdon
The Queen's Head

This Everards pub is situated in a lovely lane which curves gently towards the church. The pub lies at right angles to the lane so that the best view of the thatched 17th century building is as you enter. Across the yard there are other buildings which are part of the pub. A conservatory/dining area has been added to the main building, but this does not mar the olde worlde appearance. Inside, low beams and wooden bench seats give a cosy and historic feel to the bar. Old Original, Tiger, Beacon and Adnams ales are available, also draught cider. Drinking times: 12 noon-2.30 pm and 5 pm-11 pm weekdays, Saturday 11 am-2.30 pm and all day Sunday from 12 noon.

The pub has a restaurant and the full menu is available between 12 noon-2 pm and 5 pm-9.30 pm; Saturday 11.30 am-2 pm and 7 pm-9.30 pm; and Sunday 12 noon-2.30 pm only. A specials board lists bar food, game and fish being popular choices. There is a garden area for families, and well-behaved dogs are welcome. There is also a children's play area and Petanque Piste.

A friendly welcome awaits you, but since there are twelve Queen's Head pubs in Leicestershire make certain you get to the right one!

Telephone: Billesdon (01162) 596352.

How to get there: Billesdon is just off the A47, about 8 miles east of Leicester. The Queen's Head is in Church Street.

Parking: There is a good car park at the pub, so you can avoid parking in the narrow village streets. If you intend to walk first, please try to contact someone at the pub to seek permission to leave your car.

Length of the walk: 4 miles. Maps: OS Landranger series 141, Pathfinder SK 60/70 (GR 720026).

Billesdon is a large, compact village with many old buildings including the church and old school nearby. There are lovely street scenes with quaint thatched cottages, very well kept. Once the A47 ran straight through the village but the bypass has brought quiet now. You can see where the busy road ran by the 'ragged' edge which will, in time, recover to match the historic centre. Look for the plaque on the school wall detailing its interesting history.

The walk starts beyond the church and crosses Kate's Hill in the direction of Skeffington Vale Farm – about 1 mile of field walking. It continues via gated roads through parkland to Rolleston and back to Billesdon. There are many wide and pleasant views all round.

The Walk

Turn right from the Queen's Head into Church Street. Follow the road as it passes the school and carry on until you reach the road signs to Tur Langton and Rolleston. Ahead you will see a field gate about 100 yards further on to your left with a footpath sign.

Go into the field, which is well marked by ridge and furrow. Cross the field diagonally uphill keeping a mound to your left. This is Kate's Hill. At the far side there is a gate about 100 yards from the left hand corner of the field. Go through and into the next field. Although you may be able to walk directly across this field to the far side it will be better to follow the hedge round on your left. This brings you to a stile and plank bridge over a ditch and then onto the B6047 road to Market Harborough. Take care as you cross this road. You will find another stile opposite. When you have crossed this, keep to the high ground and aim for the left hand corner of the hedge in front. Walk with the hedge on your right towards a wooden gate ahead.

Go through and then across to follow a hedge on your right. As it bears right you keep straight on to a clump of trees in a river valley. At the far right side of the field you will find a bridle gate. Go through and then turn sharp right to a cement bridge over a stream about 30 yards away. Climb up a slope and over a broken fence into the next field. Continue uphill to the hedge on your right and follow this until just before you reach a kink in the hedge. Here there is a gap. Turn

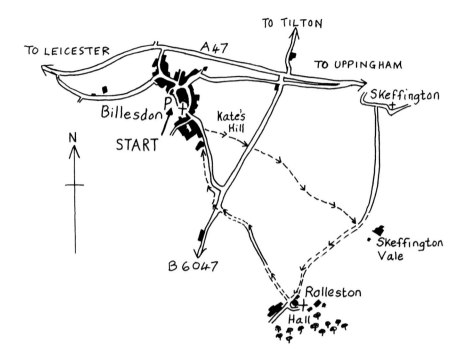

right through it and, at once, left over a fence into the next field. Cross, bearing right, to a gap in the hedge at the far side. Here, climb a fence (wire and wood) into the next field then turn left to a metal gate with a footpath sign which is also opposite the drive to Skeffington Vale Farm.

You have now reached the gated road to Rolleston. Turn right for a most pleasant walk through lovely parkland. The road has a stream and woodland to your right and you will cross two bridges. Shortly, you climb uphill to Rolleston. As you go through a metal gate into the village area you will see a signpost showing 'Gated Road to Billesdon 1½ miles' which you must eventually follow to return to your starting point.

Before you do return, go to look at the 'village'. You may have trouble finding it. Ahead of you there are some nicely converted stables, now modern housing. If you go down the Tugby Bridle Way it will lead you to the church and Tudor manor house close by. This is a lovely setting and there are walled gardens nearby. The 13th century church was rebuilt in 1740 and retains a rustic charm as you peep through the wire door to the inside. Look for the old slender stone cross in the churchyard, near the church. The hall was once a hunting seat belonging to the Master of the Quorn, later to Oswald Mosley and Viscount Churchill, who restored the church in 1899.

When you are ready, go back to the gated road to Billesdon. Did you notice the elegant street lights? The gated road is clear as it undulates in front of you. To your right look for excellent views of Skeffington Vale Farm which is most impressive. In 1 mile you reach the B6047. Turn right for 200 yards. Walk on the verge and beware of traffic here. When you reach the lane leading down into Billesdon turn left and follow this for ¾ mile into the village.

⑱ Glooston
The Old Barn

Remote this pub may be, but its friendly and warm welcome compensates for all. It is an attractively restored 16th century building at the 'end' of a small village. Opposite is a row of old cottages, and outside the pub a few old-fashioned seats where you can contemplate the church close by and the village hall. There is a small but charming restaurant, a bar, an open fire in winter, oak beams throughout and a great range of well-kept real ales on handpump – Adnams Broadside, Bateman XXXB, Flowers, Greene King IPA and Abbot, Hook Norton Old, Hookey, Mauldons Suffolk Punch, Theakston XB and Old Peculier, etc., etc. – not all available at the same time. Good wines are also available. Opening times are 12 noon-2 pm every lunchtime and 6 pm-11 pm every evening (Sunday 7 pm-10.30 pm). Bar snacks are available at all times when open. The restaurant is open Monday to Saturday, 7 pm-9.30 pm and Sunday lunchtime.

This is an award-winning pub, noted for its food, with the emphasis on fresh ingredients cooked to order. The menu changes monthly and the blackboard menu daily. Accommodation is available and you are guaranteed a good breakfast, perhaps with local ham if you wish. There is a cosy intimacy in this pub and it draws customers from many a mile to savour its attractions, so it is wise to book for meals in this excellent freehouse. Children (well-behaved ones) are allowed inside, but in summer the whole family will enjoy the picnic tables under trees and beside roses, fuschias and hanging baskets.

Telephone: East Langton (01858) 545215.

How to get there: Glooston is a small village about 12 miles south east of Leicester. It can be reached via the A6 or the A47 and the B6047 Market Harborough road. Look for signs to Glooston which is only 2 miles away from this road to the east.

Parking: There is a good car park at the Old Barn.

Length of the walk: 3 miles. Maps: OS Landranger series 141, Pathfinder SP 69/79 (GR 750958).

Glooston is a remote village and there is a sense of antiquity all around. The Roman road known as the Gartree Road runs south east from the city of Leicester (Ratae Coritanorum) and passes very close to Glooston. Though it is marked by country lanes along much of its route, on the stretch between Shangton and Medbourne – that is, in the vicinity of Glooston – only the course can be traced in the fields. A substantial Roman villa has been discovered at Glooston and part of the walk from the village to join the course of Gartree Road is probably the line of an approach road or link road used in Roman times, but now only a farm track leading nowhere in particular.

The walk proceeds across the fields to another tiny village, Stonton Wyville, where the Brudenell family lived. It then returns to Glooston alongside the stream which connects both villages and also is a headwater of the river Welland.

Writing in 1957, Professor W.G. Hoskins commented 'In twenty years' time, perhaps less, we shall have Human Reserves, oases of peace and sanity in a jet-propelled lunatic urban desert, over which no aircraft will be allowed to fly, through which no motor-car will be allowed to belch its stinking way; and when that happy day dawns the Gartree Road, from the city boundary down to Glooston, or perhaps as far as the banks of the Welland, will surely be one of the first sanctuaries to be set aside for the beleaguered little band who still value peace, quiet and country smells.'

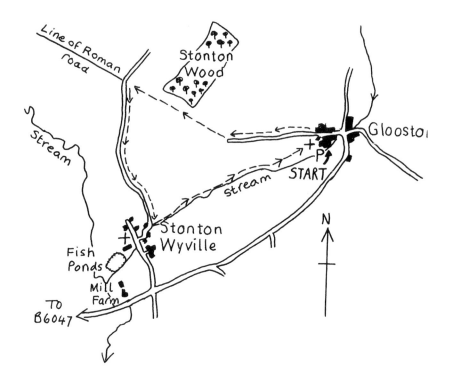

The Walk

Turn left from the Old Barn and, in a short distance, take the right fork into a wide tree-lined track which is to the right of the village hall. Do not go down the footpath next to the church – this is the way you will return.

Follow the track (sometimes muddy) and this joins the line of the old Roman road – the Gartree Road – in about ½ mile. Pass through a wooden gate here and bear right. Tur Langton church can be seen on the skyline to your left. As you proceed uphill there are fine views all round. The track is well-defined. You pass Stonton Wood on your right, and in about ½ mile go through a wooden gate into a very large pasture field with well-marked ridge and furrow. You can see diagonally to your left that a field road leads downhill to Stonton Wyville but if you require verification there is a sign indicating the direction a little further on.

Go down the field road into Stonton Wyville. This gated road has a good firm surface and soon leads into the village lane. Pause to examine the lovely chapel of St Denys, restored in 1863, with its attractive stained glass, slate tombstones and epitaphs. Note the tablet set into the south wall outside to William Brudenell dated 1636. The Brudenell family had a long connection with the village. If you can visit in harvest time you will find the chapel especially delightful.

To return to Glooston, go back down the lane leading away from the village chapel, retracing your entry to the village. At the bend in the road you will see a footpath sign which takes you alongside the stream. Go into the track near the stream, crossing several fields until you reach a rather hidden hunting gate. Go through and keep to the right edge of the field – also following the stream. A stile leads into a pasture field near to the Severn-Trent installation. Arrows mark part of this route. Then go diagonally across to Glooston church which you can just see in the trees ahead. Your path emerges at the church which is also mainly Victorian, by Joseph Goddard (1866). Now you can rest on the seats near the Old Barn.

⑲ Hallaton
The Bewicke Arms

Could one wish for a better situation for a genuine old English pub? This 400 year old thatched country inn faces the village green with its old butter cross, in probably the best of Leicestershire villages. A warm and friendly atmosphere is well backed up by efficient service and excellent food and drink. The inside may not be quite so breathtaking as the outside but the two oddly-shaped rooms – the Saddle Bar and County Room – have a real atmosphere with their old fashioned settles, some with high backs and wings, plus the decor of deer heads and farming implements. Log fires add to the greeting on cold days.

The bar food is largely home-made with help-yourself soup, daily fish specials, for example New Zealand mussels in a tasty sauce, smoked haddock and mushroom pancake, and swordfish steaks, followed by excellent lemon cheesecake. Daily specials change with the season. There is a children's menu and meal times are

12 noon-2 pm and 7 pm-9.45 pm every day. The tearoom is open from 10 am-5 pm.

Very well-kept real ales include Marston's Pedigree, Ruddles Best and County, and Webster's Yorkshire on handpump, served between 12 noon-2.30 pm and 7 pm-11 pm, Sundays 12 noon-2.30 pm. There is also Blackthorn Cider on draught.

Children can join you anywhere and there is a garden area (where dogs are welcome to wait) overlooking a pleasant valley. Picnic tables are located on this terrace. This freehouse also has accommodation.

The Bewicke Arms, which takes its name (and coat of arms) from the family who lived at Hallaton Hall until the mid-19th century, is an outstanding pub reflecting all that is best in Leicestershire.

Telephone: Hallaton (01858) 555217.

How to get there: Hallaton is a large village 17 miles east of Leicester, and just 2½ miles south of the A47 at East Norton. An alternative route is from Uppingham on the B664 via Horninghold.

Parking: The Bewicke Arms has a large car park but there is also ample street parking in the village.

Length of the walk: 5½ miles. Maps: OS Landranger series 141, Pathfinder SP 69/79 (GR 787966).

This is a beautiful part of east Leicestershire with plentiful streams, tiny valleys and well-dissected landscape. It is the area of heavy clay so boots are advisable. Do the walk on a fine day, if you can, and you will see the locality at its best.

Hallaton, in itself, could occupy half a day at least, with its duck pond, village green, butter cross, war memorial, motte and bailey castle site (one of the finest in the country), diversity of rural vernacular architecture and St Michael's church. There is an excellent small museum in Hog Lane, where you can find out about the pagan ceremony which takes place each year on Easter Monday in Hare Pie Bank, known as the Hallaton Bottle-Kicking Event. After a huge hare pie has been cut and distributed, teams from Hallaton and Medbourne (as well as anyone else who wants to take part) fight to gain possession of two wooden casks filled with ale.

The walk follows Goadby Lane for 2 miles then turns south towards Cranoe. It subsequently goes north eastwards past the lost village of Othorpe and in 1¾ miles reaches Hallaton. There are excellent views all round for much of the walk, which is largely through enormous arable fields, surely one of the best examples in Britain of 'prairie farming'.

The Walk

On leaving the Bewicke Arms, turn left to the church. As you approach note the fine 14th century broach spire and octagonal pinnacle. The whole vista must be a classic in terms of English villages.

On the edge of the stone belt, Hallaton combines marlstone, ironstone, brick and other materials in bewildering splendour. The oldest brick house appears to be 1691 and there are several 17th century timber-framed, thatched cottages. Bear right into Churchgate past a row of lovely old cottages and turn the corner with the school on your left. Bear right and do not take the footpath which you see well signed at the next bend. Instead, carry on up Goadby Lane, taking in the excellent view of the motte and bailey site on your left. Note also prolific ridge and furrow around. Soon you cross a deeply-incised valley at a ford. Should the stream be full take the route via the plank bridge. All around is heavy clay land, mostly enormous arable fields. The route is very undulating.

As you climb up a gentle ridge you eventually cross a large arable field and at the far side, to your left, you then see a yellow marker post with a blue arrow pointing into the field on your left. Turn in that direction and follow the hedge line until you reach the far right corner of this huge field where you will find a gate marked with a blue arrow. This indicates that you must go straight ahead following the hedge on your left. When this hedge turns left you must keep straight on. Do not be tempted by gates and signs on your left.

Straight in front you will find a wooden gate marked by a yellow post. Go through this gate and, again, straight ahead following the tree line and passing a small pond on your left. When you arrive at the corner of the field go through the metal gate ahead (arrow). Follow the hedge line downhill. Soon you reach a footpath sign on your right. Here you will eventually need to turn left to cross the field to find a stile and marker post at the far side. Before doing so, however, you should carry on into Cranoe to see St Michael's church opposite the Old Rectory. The base of the tower is 13th century and there is a Norman font, but storm damage in 1846 led to rebuilding in 1846-49. This village was once owned by the Brudenell family of Deene Park, Northants, better known for the Earl of Cardigan (1797-1868), the 7th Earl who led the Charge of the Light Brigade at Balaclava in 1854. He also erected the village school. There once was a Cardigan Arms in the village.

After this diversion, you have returned to the stile previously mentioned (well-signposted). Bear right alongside the hedge to Othorpe Farm which you can see ahead. At the corner of the arable field a marker post points ahead so that you follow alongside the hedge to your left, until you reach a gate at the far side into a farm paddock and a handgate in the corner. In the farmyard an arrow indicates that you must turn left until you reach a metal gate. Ahead, marker posts show your route directly across the field to double gates and a plank bridge over a stream.

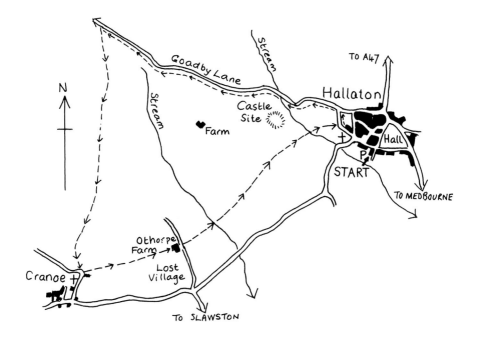

Go next to marker posts on the hill slope ahead. Here you can see the next marker post at a gap in the hedge on the far side. When you get to this point you realise that it is an open wooden handgate. Go through into a very big field but instead of taking the indicated route go diagonally across the field to the left. At the far left hand side you will see a double stile. Cross it and go on to the next yellow marker post bearing right. There is a lovely view of Hallaton from this position. At the marker post follow the arrow, bearing right, and in the distance note another post at the corner of the cemetery. At the far side of the field find a wooden stile, but before you do you must cross the stream via a plank bridge.

This is a marvellous valley for geographers – it has terracettes, cut-off meanders, ox-bow lakes, river cliffs, slip-off slopes and, to complete the scene, up-valley, in a strategic position, the motte and bailey site is located. Who could ask for anything more?

Carry on to the marker post at the corner of the cemetery and follow round the edge to reach a metal gate leading onto the village lane. Turn right to return to the centre of the village and the Bewicke Arms.

⑳ Foxton
The Black Horse

This pub was rebuilt in 1900 and is just outside the village, being opposite the church. Downhill, in a short distance, you reach the canal and the main part of Foxton. One attraction of the Black Horse is that it looks just like a large house and this is especially so when viewed from the garden at the rear. There is a patio as well, and so plenty of space outside for the visitor. Children are welcome, both inside and out.

A new conservatory restaurant extension provides excellent facilities and the home-cooked food is well-known in the area and ranges from snacks to complete meals with enough choice for all tastes. Vegetarian meals are a speciality. Booking is advisable, particularly on Sundays for lunch. Food is available 12 noon-2 pm and 7 pm-9.30 pm (9 pm on Sundays), Monday to Saturday. Drinking times are 11 am-3 pm and 6 pm-11 pm weekdays, 12 noon-3 pm and 7 pm-10.30 pm Sundays.

There is a traditional yet informal atmosphere in the pub, which serves Ansells and Tetley beers as well as Marston's traditional draught ales. In a separate building across the driveway there is a games area which includes a skittle alley, providing a focus for local entertainment. Jazz and country and western evenings are sometimes arranged. Accommodation is also available.

Telephone: East Langton (01858) 545250.

How to get there: Foxton is 4 miles north west of Market Harborough and is close to the A6. You can also approach the village via the A427, then follow signs from Lubenham.

Parking: There is a good car park to the rear of the Black Horse.

Length of the walk: 2 miles. Maps: OS Landranger series 141, Pathfinder SP 68/78 (GR 700900).

Foxton is an attractive and very interesting village situated near the Market Harborough 'arm' of the Grand Union Canal. Although most people come to see Foxton Locks, about ½ mile away from the village, this walk includes a stroll around Foxton itself to see St Andrew's church standing on a hill above the village, the famous Swingbridge and the canalside, old farmhouses and cottages, Monk Hall, the Old Court House and Baptist chapel, before a stretch along the towpath to Foxton Locks. Ascending these famous locks, which are one of the outstanding sights in Britain, the full panorama of the staircase of ten locks can be seen. The return walk is from the Bottom Lock via a country lane to the Black Horse.

The Walk

On leaving the Black Horse turn left downhill into Main Street. Go over the canal bridge, noting that once there was a blacksmith's shop here where towpath horses could be shod. Also, there was a wharf for the export of local bricks for which the village was famous. You can still see a weighbridge nearby. Turn sharp left into North Lane and then onto the canal towpath to your left. There is a sign here. Now turn left again to follow the canal towpath under the bridge you just crossed. As you walk along you pass the old school, now a field centre, originally built in 1876. You come to the Swingbridge which must be turned to allow barges to pass.

Turn left into Swingbridge Road which has several fine farmhouses and cottages, some now modernised. Look for a footpath on your left which will take you into Middle Street, near to Monk Hall. Robert Monk left the village over 70 years ago and was so successful in the hotel business in Leicester that when he died he was able to leave a large sum of money to build the Hall and set up a trust fund.

Turn right to go down to the end of Middle Street. Did you see the old mud wall on the left, often used by bees when laying their eggs in burrows which they make in the wall? At the end of the street turn

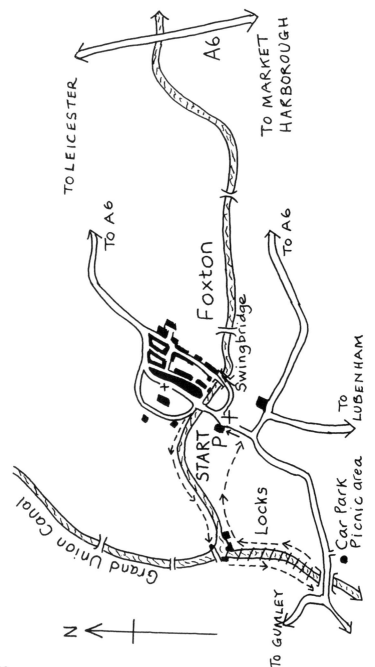

TO LEICESTER

TO A6

A6

Foxton

Swingbridge

TO MARKET HARBOROUGH

TO A6

TO LUBENHAM

START
P

Locks

Car Park
Picnic area

Grand Union Canal

N

TO GUMLEY

left round into Main Street. Look for the small village green and the Old Court House. Further down on your right is the Baptist chapel which is built of local bricks and was founded in 1716. Foxton had a strong Nonconformist element in its population at that time.

Still going down Main Street look for the Shoulder of Mutton, set back from the road in quite an imposing position. Formerly this was a farmhouse, licensed when greater business was expected due to the building of the Barge Lift. At this time, too, the Black Horse was re-built (1900).

When you reach the canal bridge again, turn right into North Lane and once more left to join the canal towpath, but this time turn right to follow it to Foxton Locks. You reach the main canal basin in just over ½ mile. This is a lovely scene to ponder on for a while. Then bear right along the towpath to cross bridge 62. Go under bridge 61 at Bottom Lock then carry on at the side of the ten locks until you reach the top, returning down the other side back to the shop and the pub at bridge 61, a freehouse with real ale as well as a fine patio where you can watch the canal activity.

Thomas Telford advised on the construction of Foxton Locks which were built between 1808 and 1814. The Market Harborough arm was opened in 1809. When the link into Northamptonshire was finally made to the Grand Junction Canal at Long Buckby, a daily service could be offered to all parts of England. Since the passage through the locks took at least one hour a quicker alternative was devised in 1900, namely an inclined plane at the side. However, due to a reduction in traffic it was dismantled in 1911, even though it had reduced the transit time to 8 minutes.

As you face the shop note the old canal notices on a wall nearby. Now turn right and cross a bridge about 50 yards away (to the right of Foxton Boat Services). Follow a rough road to the main road ½ mile away. Here there is a cemetery to your right at the corner. Turn left downhill to reach St Andrew's church on its ancient hill site. Monks may have visited here to worship as early as AD 850 since a Saxon preaching cross shaft can be seen in the church near the war memorial. The tower base and the excellent chancel were added in the early 13th century. There was restoration in 1893. In 1903 the clock which had been in use for at least 300 years was replaced and it now stands in the vestry. Look for the brass remembering the village blacksmith who sang in the choir for 27 years. This is the end of your walk as the Black Horse is opposite.

North Kilworth
The Swan

This pub is alongside a very busy road, the A427, which brings traffic from the M1 to Market Harborough. Hence it has a lively atmosphere and busy clientele. Yet behind, in the village, all is peace and tranquillity. The pub greets you with a friendly welcome.

Besides the pleasant lounge you will find a games room with pool and skittles where children are very welcome. There is an emphasis on good value home-cooked bar snacks but more substantial meals are also available, some cooked in beer. Food is obtainable from 12 noon-2 pm every day and from 7 pm-9.30 pm every evening, except Sunday. This is a Pubmaster house and has Ansells Bitter, Tetleys, Boddingtons, a guest bitter plus a wide selection of lagers and, on draught, Dry Blackthorn Cider. Drinking times are: Monday to Friday 11 am-2.30 pm and 5 pm-11 pm, Saturday 12 noon-2.30 pm and 6.30 pm-11 pm, Sunday 12 noon-2.30 pm and 7 pm-10.30 pm (Sunday lunches available). There is a covered patio in lieu of a garden area. Well-behaved dogs will be given a cautious welcome and it is best to check first if it is a good day for dogs.

Although this pub caters for the passing trade it is really the local community which gives it the lively atmosphere and settled contentment that is so obvious.

Telephone: Market Harborough (01858) 880957.

How to get there: North Kilworth is on the busy A427 Market Harborough – Lutterworth road and is only 4 miles from the M1. The Swan is on the A427 but the rest of the village lies in amazing peace to the south of it.

Parking: There is space for a few cars in front of the pub and perhaps another six or so in a small car park. Sensible parking is easily possible in the village.

Length of the walk: 5 miles. Maps: OS Landranger series 140, Pathfinder SP 69/79 (GR 616836).

North and South Kilworth are twin settlements situated on a ridge above the river Avon. Indeed, they are close to a major watershed of England with the headwaters of various streams going in the direction of the Severn, Trent and Wash.

Crossing the river is the now disused Market Harborough – Rugby railway line and, within a few yards, the Grand Union Canal. On the far side of the valley is Northamptonshire, and, indeed, part of the walk enters this county. Downriver from South Kilworth is Stanford Hall with its extensive grounds and attractive reservoir. Who could guess that these serene villages lie close to the communications heart of Britain with the junction of the M1, M6 and the A1/M1 link just 3 miles away?

The Walk

Turn right when leaving the Swan and then right again into the village lane leading to the green and war memorial. There are some stately buildings along the way, as well as the Union chapel of 1856. Turn left at the T junction past the War Memorial Hall to the church. There is excellent use of brick in this village and its rambling character leads you to many interesting discoveries and byways.

Pass through the churchyard stopping to visit St Andrew's where you will find an excellent Early English chancel and 14th century north aisle. The lower part of the tower is 14th century but the spire was heightened in 1862. Archbishop Laud was the incumbent here from 1608-1609 but it is doubtful if he was resident in the parish. Next door you will notice the old rectory, now a nursing home. Exit from the churchyard on the far side and then turn left to a sign 'Bridle Road to Welford'. Cross the cattle grid and bear right along the lane through a large field of ridge and furrow. There are wide views all around.

The track then crosses another cattle grid and continues to the left

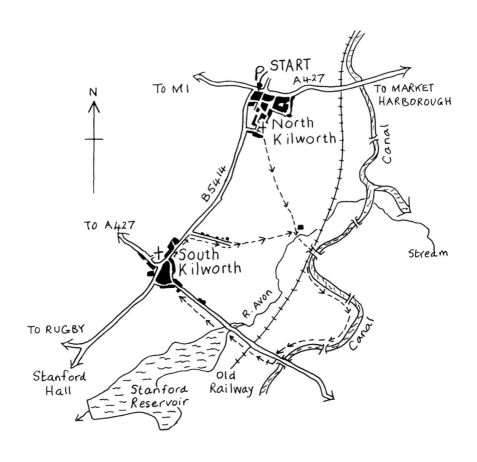

of a golf course. The spire of South Kilworth church is visible beyond the trees to your right. The track begins to go downhill steeply to the river Avon. At a metal gate to Mill Farm marked private, you take the passenger gate on the right which is marked by a yellow arrow. This leads down a narrow and sometimes muddy path to the river bridge. Note Mill Farm on your left and several signs of its antiquity. The river has meandered over the floodplain here. Who could guess that this is Shakespeare's river?

Go uphill passing the disused railway line and about 40 yards further on you reach the Grand Union Canal. You will turn right to follow the towpath, but before you do so go up onto bridge 40 for the all round view, especially to South Kilworth.

Follow the wide and grassy towpath, which is kept in good condition, past bridges 39 and 38. At bridge 37 turn right and on to the main Welford to South Kilworth road. As you ascend from under the bridge, turn left to go in the direction of South Kilworth. There is a walk of about 1 mile into the village and along the way you can see on your left Stanford Reservoir as you cross the boundary back into Leicestershire. Stanford Hall nearby was built by the Smiths of Warwick in the 1690s and contains antique furniture and fine pictures, and has lovely grounds and gardens, with a Motorcycle Museum and Percy Pilcher's 1898 Flying Machine. It is open to the public but access is via the B5414.

As you enter South Kilworth you bear right and then left to North Road. A signpost indicates 'North Kilworth 2 miles'. Turn right (unless you are in need of refreshment, when you can make a short diversion to the White Hart just round the corner to the left, or unless you would like to explore St Nicholas' church on the other side of the main road) and walk along the footpath here for about ¼ mile when you see a sign 'Bridle Road to Welford'. Turn into the track on your right known as The Belt (arrows), which also leads to an organic farm shop. When you come to the farm shop carry on straight ahead into a narrow path. This leads to a small wooden bridge and a swing gate. Go through, following the direction arrow across the golf course where an excellent and wide path has been specially laid out, but please keep to this path. At a metal gate (arrow) go through and keep to the left of the pasture field, aiming for the gate in the far corner. Go through this onto the path at Mill Farm which you walked on earlier. Turn left and retrace your steps back to the church at North Kilworth.

By the way, you may be interested to know that from 1821 to 1847 William Pearson was rector in South Kilworth. He was a founder of the Royal Astronomical Society and a noted astronomer himself. His first observatory was attached to the 18th century rectory and his later observatory can still be seen in a private house on the south side of the Kilworth – Rugby road – at least the octagonal shape. In the church there is a tablet to him which is decorated with a book, globe and telescope. In contrast, there is an epitaph in the churchyard to the local blacksmith which reads:

William Clark died 1796

'On the death of an ingenious blacksmith
My sledge and hammer lie reclin'd
My bellows to have lost their wind
My fire extinct, my forge decay'd
My voice within the dust is laid
My coals are spent, my iron gone,
My nails are drove, my work is done.'

㉒ Bitteswell
The Man-At-Arms

It is reported that the Vicar of Bitteswell, John Dowes, in 1439, left a bequest to be divided into three portions, one of which was to find and pay for a man-at-arms to join the King's army in time of war, as was required. To commemorate this act, in 1948 the name of the village pub was changed and it is the only public house of this name in the world. It is situated at one side of the village green in a very picturesque setting, with the church not far away.

Inside you will find a large L-shaped room with the lounge on entry and round the corner the snack/dining area with a low-beamed ceiling. At the far end you will see the man-at-arms himself. A full menu is available every day betwen 12 noon-2 pm and 6 pm-10 pm (Sundays all day). The menu is terrific with very reasonable prices – one of the best you will find. You can have either a snack or a complete meal supported by good wines. There is fish and sea food, Barnsley Lamb Chop, Salmon and Broccoli Mornay, and a good vegetarian choice but the pièce de resistance is the galaxy of steaks on offer including the Henry VIII Special 24 oz and the mighty Titanic 48 oz rump steak. Dishes from Mexico, Spain, Italy and China complete the vast selection. There are excellent children's choices from

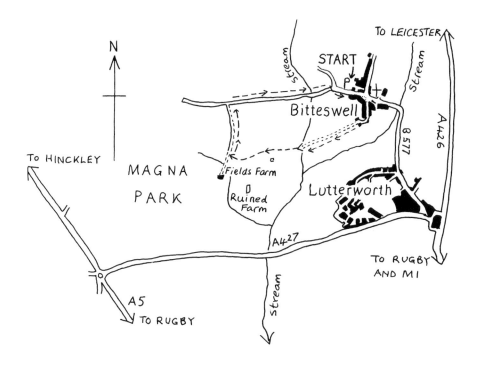

'Golden Whales', 'Chicken in the Jungle' through to vegetable nuggets.

This is a King Henry's Taverns house which serves Bass and Tetley's beers as well as Strongbow on draught. Drinking times are 11.30 am-2.30 pm and 6 pm-11 pm weekdays, Sundays all day. There is a beer garden and well-behaved dogs are welcome.

Telephone: Lutterworth (01455) 552540.

How to get there: Bitteswell is about 2 miles north west of Lutterworth which is near junction 20 on the M1 and within easy access of the A5.

Parking: There is a good car park in front of the Man-At-Arms pub, but as it gets full rather quickly please seek permission to leave your car if you are walking first and drinking later. You can park off the green if you wish, in side lanes.

Length of the walk: 3 miles. Maps: OS Landranger series 140, Pathfinder SP 48/58 (GR 538859).

Though Bitteswell lies between two very busy roads it has a lovely air of tranquillity and a pleasant arrangement of handsome houses around a spacious village green. The Hall is an 'elegant mansion' built 1838-39 and St Mary's church, though described by Pevsner as 'exceedingly dull', has a tower of about 1300 which is an essential element in the total villagescape. There was vigorous restoration in the 1880s and the lychgate is in memory of James Powell who was vicar for many years. A row of attractive almshouses known as Powell Row (1847) complements a very English scene.

The Man-At-Arms is situated alongside the green and the walk passes through part of the village then crosses the fields to a small stream, a tributary of the river Swift. In the distance is the former Bitteswell Aerodrome, now an industrial estate strategically placed next to the A5. Controversy rages about the location of a new town nearby which locals hotly dispute. The walk returns to the village along a pleasant country lane making it difficult to realise that the M1 is only 1 mile away to the east.

The Walk

On leaving the Man-At-Arms turn right to follow a narrow path next to Dunlis House, an attractive timber-framed building. Bear right round the Primary School into Valley Lane. The Royal Oak is in front of you. Go down the lane noting Stable House on your right. Ignore the footpath sign on your left at the bend. Instead, go round the bend past Shelford House with Bitteswell House on your left to the footpath sign ahead.

Go into the wide track indicated across the fields. The route is clear to follow and in the distance you see the industrial buildings on the former aerodrome. Descend into a shallow valley, with a pond on your right. At a metal gate with a concrete bridge cross into a field which is likely to be ploughed up. Go directly ahead to the right of a clump of trees where you reach a grass mound, formerly some kind of barn. Immediately to the right of this about 50 yards away there is a corner where two hedges meet. Here is a metal stile which you must cross into the next field. Walk along the hedge to your left and then bear diagonally left across to the far corner of this field. You will see the derelict buildings of Blakenhall Farm here. Do not go into this area but instead look for a gap about 100 yards away from the corner, behind you. Go through it and cross the next field where you see in front of you a farm track leading to Fields Farm (located to your left). Join the farm track and turn right to follow it until it reaches a country lane in ½ mile.

When you reach this lane turn right and follow it for 1 mile back into Bitteswell. It joins the B577 into the village.

Burbage
The Cross Keys

23

This Marston's pub is on the main street which is quite busy but has a pleasant outlook to the church with several older houses around. It is unpretentious outside but inside there is a good atmosphere and the feel of a genuine local with a darkish lounge, a snug with pew-like seats, and an open fire.

Marston's traditional ales are available, with Strongbow cider. Drinking times are 11.30 am-3 pm and 5.30 pm-11 pm weekdays, Saturdays and Sundays 11.30 am-11 pm. Bar snacks and light meals can be obtained during weekday lunchtimes. There is no pretence to haute cuisine but hunger will be well satisfied.

There is a long garden with a separate children's room and a cricket pitch at the end. Well-behaved dogs are welcome in the garden and in the pub at evening time.

Telephone: Hinckley (01455) 239443.

How to get there: Burbage is in south west Leicestershire only 2 miles away from Watling Street (the A5) and the M69 is even closer via the A5070. Hinckley and Burbage are situated very near to each other in the triangle made by the A5 and the M69, the Leicester – Birmingham railway line dividing the two places.

Parking: No pub car park, but there is good street parking close to the church and in nearby streets.

Length of the walk: 4½ miles. Maps: OS Landranger series 140, Pathfinder SP 49/59 (GR 442928).

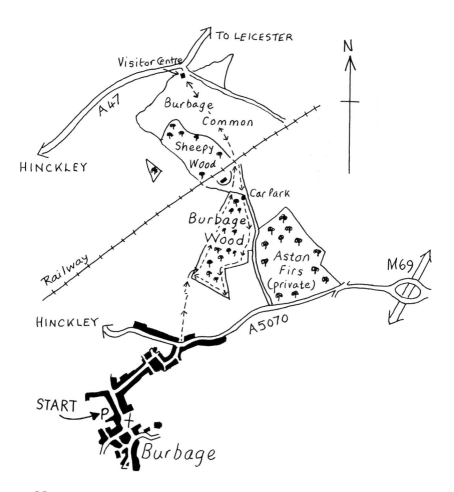

According to W.G. Hoskins 'Burbage is a most interesting place to explore: it was once a flourishing little country town, now overshadowed by Hinckley two miles away, and it contains a good deal of praiseworthy building from the late 16th to the mid-19th century, especially in and around the broad street by the church'.

As part of the town's interesting past, the landscape just to the north has two valuable features: Burbage Wood and Burbage Common, both as significant and important as the fine old buildings in the town. They are 200 acres (80 ha) in area including woodland, scrub and grassland with a rich variety of flora and fauna. There are two natural woodlands – Burbage Wood and Sheepy Wood containing oak, ash, maple with hazel below, probably the remnants of the medieval Hinckley Forest. They are still managed by coppicing which you can usually see on your walk. The common was owned by the manorial estate and commoners could graze livestock on it by right. It is rich in plants and animals. In damper places marsh forget-me-not and ragged robin thrive, whilst in better drained soils there is spiny restharrow, lesser stitchwort and tormentil. It is favoured by butterflies such as the orange-tip and comma. Kestrels hover above and whitethroats and meadow pipits breed there.

There is a network of routes through both woods and common and the area is popular – but there is room for all. Our walk starts in Burbage and passes through estates before reaching the A5070 in ½ mile. Thence it penetrates Burbage Wood and goes under the railway line, making for the Visitor Centre at the far side of the common. The return is via a different path through the woods. All routes are most pleasant, easy, level and contrasting as well as being well waymarked.

The Walk

Turn left on leaving the Cross Keys and walk on for about 300 yards until you reach Woodland Avenue on your right. Go down this road to Meadow Drive, turning left and then right. Bear right again into Winchester Road and now carry on to the A5070. Cross this road carefully to a sign opposite, 'Burbage Woods & Common'.

Go through a gap between the buildings to a metal gate. Climb the stile at the side into the pasture field. Walk along the hedge and in about 150 yards you will see a stile on your left. Cross this into the field, turning sharp right to follow the hedge. At the corner of this field you turn right across a stile into Burbage Wood. Turn left and keep to the edge of the wood. Ignore pathways, however important they may look, to your right. Soon you reach the end of the wood and go through a wooden handgate, across a plank bridge into a rough meadow. Go straight ahead to the railway bridge you will see. To your left is Woodhouse Farm which sometimes provides refreshments.

Go under the railway bridge and keep between two blue marker posts ahead. You are now on the common and if you go straight ahead you will arrive at the Visitor Centre in ½ mile. This houses a display (free of charge) interpreting the site, as well as a souvenir shop. Guided walks and talks are available from time to time.

When you are ready you can return by the same route to the railway bridge. If you prefer, however, there are several different paths which will bring you to the same point, for example, one is through Sheepy Wood. Information boards will give further details.

As you return under the railway bridge go towards the left hand corner of the pasture field. Follow the stream along, which is on your left. You then see blue marker posts indicating a lane – Smithy Lane. Close by there are picnic tables. Cross a plank bridge into a small car park. At the far left side there is a small handgate. Turn right through it, over a wooden bridge into the wood. Turn left along a woodland path and at a path crossroads keep straight on. At a T junction turn right. Follow this path, but then bear left keeping on the edge of the wood. When the path bears right you will see the spire of Burbage church to your left.

Carry on to a stile at the corner of the wood in front of you, keeping to the left of a litter bin. This is the same stile by which you entered the wood earlier on. Cross it and turn left to follow along the hedgeside. When you reach the stile on your left which leads into the pasture field where you first started, cross it and make you way back to the A5070. Return via Winchester Road, Meadow Drive and Woodland Avenue to the centre of Burbage.

Sibson
The Cock Inn

24

Situated on a corner, this pub is both attractive and interesting outside and inside. This is an old building dating from 1250 and it was owned by the church until 1939. Its first full licence was granted in 1954. The thatch, black/white timbering, lattice windows and low doorways all reveal its age as does the wattle and daub wall inside and the lovely small, low-beamed rooms. There are snug places for everyone it seems, all tucked away very nicely. All around one is aware of antiquity. There are seats outside at the back to make use of on fine days, as well as tables on a patio.

The popular Stable Restaurant has both à la carte and table d'hôte menus and specialises in all kinds of mouth-watering dishes which are home-made. The bar menu includes steak and kidney pie, honey roast ham, Scottish steaks grilled to taste, and there are also children's dishes. These are all available between: 11.30 am-2 pm and 6.30 pm-9.45 pm weekdays, Sundays 12 noon-2 pm (no bar meals, Sunday lunch only) and 7 pm-9.30 pm (restaurant closed on Sunday night). Children are welcome in the eating area and restaurant. This is a Punch Taverns house with well-kept Bass, M&B Brew XI, a variety of lagers and Strongbow and Woodpecker cider. Drinking times are 11.30 am-2.30 pm and 6.30 pm-11 pm weekdays, Sundays 12 noon-3 pm and 7 pm-10.30 pm. There is piped music and a games machine.

You would be wise to do the walk first as once you are established inside this lovely old pub you may not want to leave in a hurry.

Telephone: Tamworth (01827) 880357.

How to get there: Sibson is in the far west of the county about 18 miles away from Leicester. In fact, it is nearer to Tamworth. Market Bosworth is about 4 miles to the north east. From the West Midlands the best approach is via the M42 joining the A5 at junction 10 and then turning onto the A444. From Coventry and Nuneaton it is easy to travel along the A444. From Leicester one suitable and scenic route is via Desford and Market Bosworth to the A444.

Parking: There is excellent parking at the Cock Inn.

Length of the walk: 5½ miles. Maps: OS Landranger series 140, Pathfinder SK 20/30 (GR 355009).

This walk is in the pleasantly undulating claylands of West Leicestershire, in the vicinity of the Roman Watling Street and quite close to the river Sence which joins the river Anker near King Dick's Hole, just beyond Ratcliffe Culey. The famous Twycross Zoo is only about 5 miles north of Sibson along the A444.

The route is rectangular, crossing the fields from Sibson to Sheepy Parva, then over the Sence at the old mill to Sheepy Magna, going south to Ratcliffe Culey and following the country lane east until again crossing the fields on a rural short cut with Sibson in sight on a hill. Be prepared for some mud as you pass near streams.

All three villages (four with Sheepy Parva) have points of interest and some good buildings. The churches are certainly worth looking into, for example, at Ratcliffe Culey the early 14th century church has a moated homestead site to the south east, whilst at Sheepy Magna there is a fine medieval tithe barn at Newhouse Grange, ½ mile to the north west. Ratcliffe Culey means the red cliff or bank held by Hugo de Culy in 1285 and Sheepy may mean a dry island where sheep might safely graze. Just a few miles south of this walk is the Roman settlement of Mancetter – at least the site of it. You can see that though this may seem a neglected area to some, it has many secrets for you to discover on the walk.

The Walk

Leave the Cock Inn via the front door and turn left into the village lane. If you are parked in the pub car park go out into the village lane also turning left. Proceed down the lane until you reach the right-angled bend. Look for Glenfield Cottage and Vine Cottage on your left. The pathway is between the two and you must

102

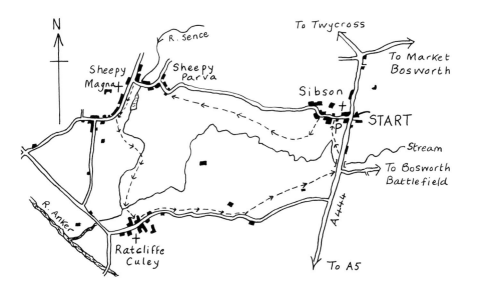

enter a handgate to Glenfield Cottage, then follow the path behind the houses, bearing left until you reach a stile.

Keep the hedge on your right and go over another stile. Go straight ahead across a field to a telegraph pole following the line of a fence. At a yellow mark on one of the poles go through a gate and follow a hedge line. Cross a plank bridge at a yellow marker turning into a gate on your right. Then follow the hedge on your left to a yellow marker post near a barn. Cross a stile into a ploughed field and go across to the far side to the left of some trees. With the trees on your right go to a marker post ahead. At the next post go diagonally right to a telegraph post and the next yellow marker. Turn left to cross a stile. Keep to the hedge on your left following the line of telegraph poles. Cross a plank bridge and go ahead to the next stile and plank bridge.

Now Sheepy Parva comes into view ahead and the way is clear across three stiles, each with an arrow. The telegraph poles veer off to the left away from you. Go ahead to a metal gate which leads onto a country lane. Turn left and follow it round passing Moat House on your left. Turn left into Mill Lane (B585). Carry on and you will turn into Sheepy Magna. After crossing a large Mill Pond you turn sharp left into the village street where you will find a post office, a shop, the Black Horse and the church.

In ¼ mile, as you begin to leave the village centre, look for a sign on the left side of the lane 'Footpath to Ratcliffe Culey'. Go over the stile (arrow) here and cross to a yellow marker post ahead. Follow the stream round a little but then turn in a 2 o'clock direction to another post on the far side of the field. Cross the bridge here and turn right to follow the stream. At the river bend climb a double stile and plank bridge (arrow). Cross the field to the far right corner (marker post). Ratcliffe Culey is ahead on a ridge. Cross a stile and follow the hedge on your right to a wooden bridge at the far side. Then go ahead uphill towards the church spire. You arrive at a farmyard behind some village houses. Go over a fence into a green track between the houses and you come to the village street with a red telephone box opposite you.

Turn left to walk along the lane leading from Ratcliffe to the A444 for 1 mile. Just beyond Barn Farm, on your right, look for a footpath pole. This is the route across the fields to Sibson which you can see on a ridge in the distance. Its church is distinctive.

Cross the stile here and follow the hedge on your left to a yellow marker post in the corner. Cross this stile and then go diagonally right across a large field to a post in the far hedge. Go through a gap then through a gate opposite across to a yellow post at the rear of a farmhouse. Cross a stile and plank bridge going ahead to the next stile. Turn left and follow the hedge on your right to the next post and stile behind the farm. Cross and go to the left of a pond towards the next post and stile ahead. Cross to the stile and plank bridge opposite, keeping the hedge on your left. You arrive at the gate to a bungalow. This is the right of way and you are permitted to go through it then onto a farm drive bearing right to the main road (A444).

Turn left and keep to the verge. Cross the bridge where you see the sign to Sibson. After about 100 yards you come to a footpath sign on your left, just before reaching Miller's Hotel. Cross the stile here (arrow) and bear right diagonally to the far corner. The stream is on your left. Cross a stile and follow the new fencing to the village ahead – the church is in front of you and soon you arrive at a metal gate. Follow the road between an estate of palatial houses and at the village lane turn right to arrive back at the Cock Inn.

㉕ Stoney Cove
The Cove

This is an extraordinary location for a pub. An attractive leafy lane leads to an undistinguished building which sits below a towering quarry face and all around the sides of the quarry seem to engulf the little cabin. In the centre of the quarry is a very deep lake, now the setting for the National Diving Centre and water sports, but once a working quarry into the valuable igneous rocks which also occur at other locations in the area such as Enderby, Narborough, Croft and Sapcote. As the walk shows, Croft is still a working quarry.

Inside The Cove, a large and comfortable lounge has several cosy corners and there is a very long bar which usually means you are served quickly. There are lanterns, charts, ship emblems and other nautical artefacts and in the ceiling a ship's wheel. A dining section is a no-smoking area. The paved balconies allow good views of events on the lake, and are very popular with children. As there is no garden, please leave your dog, however well behaved, outside in the car.

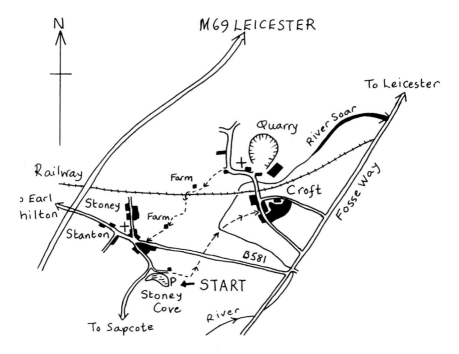

The real ales are Tetley Bitter and draught Burton Ale with Ansells and Calders available. Scrumpy Jack is on draught, as is Guinness. There is a very good range of lagers, non-alcoholic drinks and I think I saw Strongbow Cider just round the bar corner. Drinking times are 11 am-2.30 pm and 6.30 pm-11 pm weekdays, 12 noon-3 pm and 7 pm-10.30 pm Sundays (11 am-11 pm on bank holidays and Saturday and Sunday during British summertime). This is a freehouse and the food is good and varied with a specials board every day. The famous Yorkshire pudding with appropriate fillings is available. Prices are reasonable and custom busy, very busy at weekends and in summertime. Food times are 11.30 am-2 pm (to 2.30 pm Saturday and Sunday) and 7 pm-9.30 pm. When the pub is open all day, food is available all day too.

Telephone: Hinckley (01455) 274198.

How to get there: Stoney Cove is near to Stoney Stanton. Follow the sign to Sapcote from Stoney Stanton. Both villages are about 10 miles south west of Leicester, quite close to the M69. You can approach from Hinckley via the A5070 and B4069. The A5 is also close and you can take the B4114 to Sharnford and Sapcote if you approach from this direction. From Leicester take the A46 and B4114.

Parking: Strictly, the pub itself has no car park but customers are able to use the very extensive area alongside the lake all the way up to the pub, and it is unusual to find this completely occupied by diving teams, etc.

Length of the walk: 5½ miles. Maps: OS Landranger series 140, Pathfinder SP 49/59 (GR 496941).

This is a walk into Leicestershire's industrial past. Starting at Stoney Cove, once a thriving quarry area known as Lane's Hill, including Top Quarry and Stanton Top Pit, the walk crosses the river Soar as it makes a sharp right-angled bend on its way to flow through central Leicester. Close by, ½ mile to the east is the old Roman road known as the Fosse Way, later the A46. No doubt the Romans were the first to quarry the roadstone nearby. In the distance Croft Hill can be seen, a regional focus. You will see the present quarry areas from your walk. Note also the charming stream and church as you reach Croft. You then cross the fields for 1½ miles until you arrive at Stoney Stanton where you go through the village to return to Stoney Cove.

The Walk

Walk out of Stoney Cove along the lane by which you first entered. At the main road turn right into the bridlepath signposted. As you follow this path you have good views of the Cove to your right. Go through a metal gate at the farm and then bear right along a cinder track to a telegraph pole where the track ends. Now turn left at the edge of the field and carry on to a handgate in the opposite corner of the next field. Go through and onto a cinder path which leads to the main road (arrow). To your left is the village of Stoney Stanton. Cross the road carefully to the bridlepath sign opposite. As you go through the metal gate here beware that it does not fall on your foot as it partly collapses when opened. Walk straight ahead then bear slightly right to a gate at the far corner of the next field. Go through this metal gate, keeping the hedge on your left, making for a gap in the hedge at the corner of the field with a bridge beyond.

Cross the footbridge via a handgate (arrow) and over the arched stone bridge. This is the river Soar. Follow the hedgeline as it curves ahead of you on a wide grass track. Croft Hill can be seen in front. The track leads clearly into Croft village, via several gates. As it comes to a lane you walk down this to the main road and turn left, then over a railway bridge with views to the huge complex of ECC Quarries on your right. Beware of lorry traffic on this stretch on working days. Cross the pretty stream then turn left uphill with the Heathcote Arms opposite making a lovely scene. As you walk up Huncote Road keep to the upper pathway. Follow the road round past the church on the right. Go round the bend but turn left at the footpath sign just beyond the house. You are in a narrow path here.

Keep to the right of the cemetery gate, cross the stile and go diagonally to the far left corner. Cross a fence and concrete bridge over a small stream then follow a raised track towards a farmhouse. Go through the metal gate to the left of the farmhouse then turn left under the railway. Go straight ahead with the hedge on your right for about 250 yards. Look for the gap/fence in the hedge here. Turn right to cross this under the pylons. You need to aim for the far left corner of this field with Stoney Stanton church spire as a landmark ahead. You may find it easier to walk round the field boundary rather than across.

When you reach the corner cross a deep ditch and fence. Go diagonally to a gate at the far corner. Turn right through this gate into a muddy farm track. Although the right of way is over a stile on the left and then following parallel to the farm drive it may be permissible for you to use the drive, as it is actually running unfenced in the same field. At any rate, the right of way joins the drive as it leads into a village lane and then the main road, where you turn right. Keep to the footpath, turning left at the crossroads signposted to Sapcote. Go down this road until, in a short distance, you reach the entry to Stoney Cove. Follow this lane back to your starting point.

㉖ Newtown Linford
The Bradgate

The inn is situated along the main street of Newtown Linford within just 200 yards of the entrance to Leicestershire's premier beauty spot, Bradgate Park. The pub's exterior is typical of the village and the Charnwood area with its sturdy granite construction, and presents a fine frontage to the street. To the rear there is a family garden play area and a large beer garden. Inside there is a long bar and main lounge area which has recently been stylishly refurbished to very high standards. There are discoveries to be made on a first visit, since there seem to be many different sections to this deceptively large building.

You have an outstanding selection of traditional cask ales with Everards Tiger Best Bitter, Original Premium Cask Ale and Beacon Bitter as well as a regular guest, and seasonal ales. There is also a comprehensive range of lagers, smooth ales, ciders and stouts. An extensive wine list is available, either by the bottle or the glass.

Pub opening times are: Monday to Saturday 11 am-11 pm, Sunday 12 noon-10.30 pm. Food is served: Monday to Thursday 12 noon-3 pm and 6 pm-9 pm, Friday 12 noon-3 pm and 6 pm-10 pm, Saturday 12 noon-4 pm and 6 pm-10 pm, Sunday 12 noon-4 pm and 6 pm-9 pm. There is a full restaurant and bar menu, plus a wide range of snacks are available throughout the day. Chef's daily specials are reasonably priced and feature an array of temptingly different alternatives. During the summer months barbecues are a popular feature at the Bradgate.

This is one of Everards best known and popular pubs due to its character and history. It is very conventiently located, being adjacent to Bradgate Park and easily accessible from the M1.

Telephone: Markfield (01530) 242239.

How to get there: Newtown Linford is about 6 miles north west of Leicester and can be reached via the B5327 Anstey road which is accessed from the A46 Leicester by-pass. Alternatively leave the M1 at Junction 22 and follow signs to Bradgate Park from the A511.

Parking: Although there is ample parking at the rear of the pub, it is shared on occasions with the village hall across the road. At these times, the car park can become rather congested and it would probably be a good idea to 'phone the Bradgate prior to your walk.

Length of the walk: 3½ miles. Maps: OS Landranger series 129, Pathfinder SK 41/51 (GR 519100).

The spectacular scenery of Charnwood Forest is a sharp contrast to the flat plains and valleys of the Midlands. It has been likened to a 'Little Switzerland' or a miniature Wales. Rocky crags formed out of some of Britain's oldest strata punctuate the skyline and eminences such as Bardon Hill, Old John and Beacon Hill are very well-known to local people. One of the outstanding parts of Charnwood is Bradgate Park, near Newtown Linford. The river Lin traverses the park and passes the ruins of Bradgate House, once the home of Lady Jane Grey, the nine days' Queen of England. Deer roam the park and horses, cattle, sheep and rabbits have grazed the area and still do. There is much bracken – perhaps too much – and this has to be controlled by burning and bruising. Heather has been re-introduced in the hope that it may flourish again. There are spinneys and plantations, many pines, but it is the pollarded oaks which catch the eye. The story remains that they were beheaded in memory of Lady Jane Grey.

The walk starts at the Bradgate and you should not neglect Newtown Linford itself, for this linear village contains a variety of vernacular houses and farms which demonstrate the uses of local building materials excellently. There are also many instances of timber-framed buildings with plaster and brick infilling. Indeed, Bradgate House was one of the first buildings in Britain to use brick, along with nearby Kirby Muxloe castle. The curve of the street and attractiveness of buildings makes this a memorable village scene.

Soon the walk enters Bradgate Park and follows the river Lin passing the ruins of Bradgate House, moving alongside Cropston Reservoir, then round Coppice Plantation, across to Old John via Sliding Stone Wood and back to the entrance

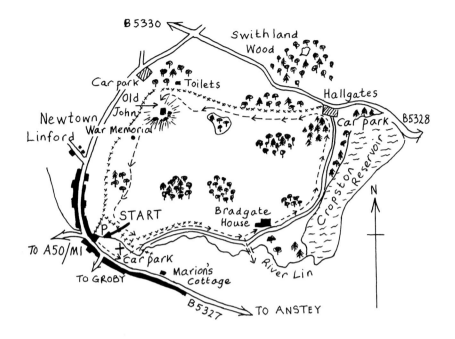

downhill passing Tyburn. You should look inside Marion's Cottage as you go out where there are displays about the park and many publications.

The Walk

On leaving the Bradgate turn left down the main street. You pass the church on your left. If time allows, go inside to see the odd ABCD tombstone which is about 15 ins by 3 ft. It has no name, only the letters of the alphabet in both capitals and small letters with two incomplete sets of Arabic numerals. Once it stood in the churchyard but was moved inside and attached to the wall behind the font. The origin is still a mystery.

Turn left into the car park leading into Bradgate Park and cross through the kissing gate to the road beyond. Follow the river as it passes through its 'gorge' section known as Little Matlock. Here the massive intrusive igneous rock contrasts with siltstones which you can see if you go over the bridge opposite the house ruins, into Stable Pit. Note the red clay river cliff from which it is supposed the bricks for the house were made. Return to the main path and you can have a closer look at Bradgate House, completed in 1502 for the Grey family. It is one of the earliest unfortified grand houses in England. Follow the road alongside the Cropston Reservoir – part of the Victorian water

111

supply scheme for Leicester and opened in 1870.

Just before you reach the Hallgates car park, which is another entry/exit to Bradgate, go over to the crags at the edge of Coppice Plantation. Here you will see evidence of Charnwood's volcanic past. There are fine grained rocks of volcanic dust cleaved and hardened into slates – looking zig-zagged in appearance. Now you should turn left round the plantation making for Old John. There are several routes possible and you can take your choice. However, if you bear left around Sliding Stone Wood you will, on your course there, pass through some of the original moorland of Charnwood – wet heath and bog. The crags in the wood indicate further volcanic material, this time agglomerates and solidified ash and dust heavily contorted and twisted.

Go on to Old John, a folly built in 1786, to commemorate an old retainer who was killed on the spot when a maypole fell on him at a coming of age party for the Earl of Stamford's relative. The beermug shape is alleged to reflect Old John's partiality for ale. Savour the view, and use the toposcope as this is the highest point in the park. Can you see Leicester? Belvoir Castle? Billesdon Coplow? Surely this outcrop will confirm the idea of Charnwood as a major volcanic area over 600 million years ago.

Consider too, from your viewpoint, that Bradgate was a medieval deer park and though much altered, even yet it conveys that sense of an ancient landscape. The danger today is that too many feet will erode pathways causing soil loss, and so careful management of the park is necessary so that the past can be conserved realistically, whilst allowing us to continue to enjoy it.

You can follow any route you choose back to the entrance but you might prefer to go past the war memorial then downhill to a clump of trees known as Tyburn, and thence to the car park. From there (don't forget Marion's Cottage to the left) turn right to return to the Bradgate.

Mountsorrel
The Waterside Inn

Also known as the inn on the lock, the Waterside Inn was built 200 years ago when the Grand Union Canal came through from Loughborough to Leicester. It is situated next to the lock with the old humped-back bridge close by and lots of canal traffic to watch from the beer garden and patio fronting onto the canal. This is a long building and the extension to the lounge took in the old stables where bargees kept their horses. Until 1965 the pub was known as the Duke of York. As you sit in the lounge not only do you have a fine view of the lock but also of the castle hill behind Mountsorrel. When you emerge at the rear you look across the flat valley of the river Soar towards Sileby, a village situated above the flood levels.

This is an Everard's house with its very special Everards Old Original, and Strongbow draught cider. Drinking times are: weekdays 11.30 am-2.30 pm and 6 pm-11 pm, Sundays 12 noon-3.30 pm and 7 pm-10.30 pm (open all day Sundays from Easter to September). The food is very good value and served most efficiently and quickly. The menu is basic and good, with a normal, everyday look to satisfy people in a hurry and the passing trade, since this pub is very well situated for valley cross-traffic. Food is available every day from 12 noon-1.45 pm

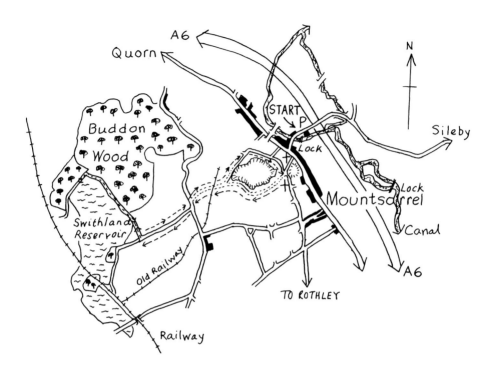

and 7 pm-9 pm (on Sundays from Easter to September, food is available 12 noon-8 pm). The full menu is there at all times and some of its highlights are sirloin or rump steaks, gammon, mixed grill, home-made steak and mushroom pie, and a traditional roast is available at lunchtime on Sunday. A selection of wines is listed and children's half portions are available at half price. Children are welcome, especially in the garden area, and although there is no family room, the lounge is very long and there is plenty of space. Well-behaved dogs are also welcome in the bar.

Telephone: Leicester (01162) 302758.

How to get there: Mountsorrel is 6 miles north of Leicester, very close to the A6. The nearest junction on the M1 is 23, then following the A512 and the A6.

Parking: There is a large car park at the Waterside Inn and a field next to the pub where you can leave your car while you walk, but beware the narrow road leading to it and the hump-backed bridge.

Length of the walk: 5 miles. Maps: OS Landranger series 129, Pathfinder SK 41/51 (GR 582152).

There are some splendid walks around Mountsorrel, but, too often, the floodwaters of the river Soar fill the intervening valley between Sileby and Barrow on the far side and Mountsorrel on the other. Hence, this walk explores the firmer ground to the west of the village, which is compressed between the fine castle site and the river, now canalised as part of the Grand Union Canal. Along this route ran the Leicester to Derby road. For a great deal of time the village remained linear but has now expanded in its southern section towards Rothley Plain. The castle stood on granite or Mountsorrel Syenite as it is more properly known. This has been the key to the development of the village. Most buildings are constructed of it and so are the setts on the ground. The canal was the export point and at Jelly's Wharf it could be sent 'to any part of the Kingdom'. In this district were three almost indestructible materials: Mountsorrel granite, Swithland slate and Barrow lime mortar.

This walk will delight those who like to ramble amongst the industrial graveyards of England. First you see one of the finest views in the Midlands from the castle hill. Then you pass one of the largest former granite quarries in the country, now a landfill site. Then across the course of an old railway and soon to Swithland Reservoir, built in 1896 along with several other 19th century reservoirs in Charnwood, to supply Leicester. Nearby you pass Buddon Wood, once fought over by environmentalists to save it from mineral exploitation but now one of the biggest 'holes in Europe'.

The Walk

From the Waterside Inn turn left and over the hump-backed bridge taking great care about the traffic here. There are lots of interesting things to see on river and canal and nearby is the Soar Valley Boatyard as well as many longboats moored at Mountsorrel Lock.

At the main road (once the A6, which now bypasses the town) turn left and cross into Watling Street on the opposite side. Go uphill noting the derelict buildings en route and also the profuse use of granite. Just before the road bears right go up some steps which lead to the castle hill. There are superb views all across the county from here. There may have been a Roman temple on this site and the Norman castle lasted until, by order of Henry III, it was destroyed because it was 'a nest of the devil and a den of thieves and robbers'. Return to the lane and carry on along it, passing Poplar House at the corner and bearing right. When you reach the T junction go straight ahead into a trackway. You are still in an eminent position and can see the second of Mountsorrel's churches to your left. Note the large granite boulders along the edge of your track.

As you bear right you are following round one of Britain's former largest quarries, now a landfill site. Keep away as it is dangerous, but, from time to time you do get glimpses of the rock face. Continue along the track until you reach a lane with a seat on the left. Here you turn left and cross an old railway bridge. The line formerly went south west to join the Great Central Railway (now operated as a vintage steam railway). To your right is an area of scrub and bracken.

On reaching a more major road you see a sign opposite, 'Rushey Lane'. Cross over to this but turn left along the main road until you arrive at Kinchley Lane on the right in about 100 yards. Turn down this lane until you reach gates marking private land of the Severn-Trent Water Authority. Follow the road round to the right until you reach the Swithland Reservoir dam. From this vantage point you can see the whole reservoir and, in the distance, the viaduct of the Great Central Railway. Unfortunately, because Buddon Wood is private land and actively being quarried we cannot return by this route. This illustrates the land-use conflicts between mineral exploitation and other users.

We must, therefore, return by the same route. When you reach the junction of Kinchley Lane and the main road turn left and go about 100 yards to turn right into the lane from which you emerged earlier in the walk. Go down this lane but do not go back into your original track. Instead bear left and carry on until you reach the approach to the landfill site. Here there are several notices and white blocks to limit traffic, but you can walk through without any trouble. Thus you turn right through the approach road and go straight ahead until you see a tree-lined track in front. This also has two white stone blocks on it. Pass through and walk on until you reach the top end of Watling Street, close to your original start along the track. You should recognise this point. The castle hill is just ahead.

Turn left downhill until you are at the main village road, then turn left to reach the Sileby road in a short distance, on your right. This returns you to the Waterside Inn. If time allows you might look around Mountsorrel village. According to Hoskins it is 'well-worth exploring on foot for devotees of English regional styles'. It has been called an 'unkempt little town' but it has some fine buildings such as the elegant 18th century facade near the Sileby road corner and the domed rotunda which replaced the medieval cross. Once the town was an important market with a famous 8-day fair and in the 18th century the hosiery trade flourished. The discerning eye can still see evidence of this memorable past, indeed Hoskins illustrates one of the finest examples of peasant building dated 1705, as a farmhouse in the main street.

If you wish to shorten this walk you can complete the circle as the map shows without going on to Swithland Reservoir. This reduces the walk to 2 miles.

28 Copt Oak
The Copt Oak Inn

This was always a meeting place. Here several forest parishes and manors met, here the Swanimote Court of Groby Manor was held under a great oak tree (Copt Oak means either 'top oak' or 'pollarded oak'), reputed to have been behind the church but blown down in a gale in 1855. Now the M1 slashes through Charnwood Forest and a multitude of other roads join to provide a constant hum of traffic.

The old pub, just beyond the church, has been completely modernised and it is very attractive and spacious both outside and inside. Inside there is a huge dining area and many pleasant sections to enjoy a good drink in a sumptuous atmosphere, with a very long bar enabling quick and efficient service. This is a Marston's Tavern Tables pub with the usual range, including Pedigree and Scrumpy Jack and Woodpecker cider on draught. A no-smoking area is provided. Drinking times are 11.30 am-11 pm Monday to Saturday, and 12 noon-10.30 pm on Sunday. There is a very good lawn with tables outside for all the family, including dogs, who must remain there, however well behaved. There is a good choice of food, ranging from bar snacks to the specials board, which is available between 12 noon and 10 pm Monday to Saturday and on Sundays from 12 noon-9.30 pm.

Although the pub is near a busy junction you can still savour the tranquillity of Charnwood by stepping on this walk which takes you behind the church and soon leaves the 20th century for more pastoral scenes. Before you leave the pub don't forget to take in the view to Bardon Hill, Leicestershire's highest point at over 900 ft.

Telephone: Markfield (01530) 242353.

How to get there: The most direct route is the M1 leaving at junction 22 and using the B591 or the B587 to reach Copt Oak. From Leicester take the A50; from Loughborough, the B5350.

Parking: There is an excellent car park at the Copt Oak Inn.

Length of the walk: 4½ miles. Maps: OS Landranger series 129, Pathfinder SK 41/51 (GR 482130).

There are some outstanding views on this walk though the centre of it consists of the gentle valley of the Ulverscroft Brook. About half the walk is along two country lanes and the rest across fields or alongside woodland. Be ready for muddy points and undulating scenery.

After walking down Whitcroft Lane with its noteworthy 19th century houses, you will go through the lovely Ulverscroft valley, past the ruined Priory. This was an Augustinian foundation of 1150. Only about 4 miles to the north west is the living monastery of Mount St Bernard which you can visit later.

From the magical ruins of Ulverscroft you pass the Earl of Stamford's pond which he re-excavated in about 1860 to improve his shooting and fishing. This was very likely to have been the fishpond of the Priory. You skirt round Poultney Wood with fine views to left and right, past a nature reserve and back to Copt Oak.

The Walk

Turn right out of the pub car park and then right again to walk up to St Peter's church, which was built in 1837, but looks older due to the sombre granite used. Go round the back of the church to a yellow marker post then over a stile in the wall (arrow). As you approach the radio masts turn left to a stile (arrow), cross into a field and keep to the left side until you reach the stile at the far left corner. The masts that you see were moved from Bardon Hill as quarrying there was interfering with reception. Climb over the stile and follow the wall ahead keeping to the left of it. Aim for a gap in the hedge in front. Go over the fence here and turn right into Whitcroft Lane. Walk along the

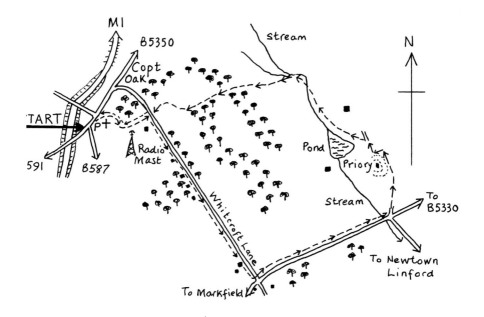

lane for about ½ mile passing a nature reserve entrance, 'Tree Tops'
and several other buildings. You will see many fine cottages and
houses, especially when you reach the crossroads where Polly Bott's
Lane joins. Here the Leicester born architect and furniture designer
Ernest Gimson built a series of Ulverscroft houses for members of his
family, some of which you can see from the crossroads or nearby, for
example, Lea Cottage, built in 1900, thatched and whitewashed,
Rockyfield with its lovely gardens, built in 1908, and Stoneywell
Cottage built in 1899 – all with unusual features reflecting the 19th
century Arts and Craft Movement.

At the crossroads turn left and when you have walked another ½
mile you reach the farm track on the left leading to Ulverscroft Priory.
This is opposite to the lane to Newtown Linford. Turn left into the
farm track. You pass the moat and Prior's Lodge, in active use in the
13th century, now a house with the bridge nearby. Continue as the
track turns left and right then crosses a cattle grid, keeping to the wall
bordering the pond. Ignore private notices here as this is a genuine
right of way. As you reach the corner of the field a waymark directs
you straight ahead to a jutting-out section of woodland and stream on
your left.

Look on your left for a footbridge and cross it into the woodland.
Then you can walk along a clearly-defined pathway to your right as
it follows the edge of the wood with a nature reserve sign on your left.

Now go over a footbridge into a field and then to the next wood. At the field corner a footpath sign next to a wooden gate directs you along the side of the wood via a wire fence. Walk with the wood on your left and pastureland to your right until you reach a footpath sign high on a tree and a wooden handgate on the left. Go through this gate and a good path leads through the wood to another gate at the far side.

Go through the gate into a field. You see the radio masts ahead and behind lovely views over your route. Keep the wood on your left and continue uphill through a wooden farm gate then follow a stone wall round bearing right to a wooden handgate. Pass through and follow the fenced track until you reach the stile which brings you back to Whitcroft Lane. As you emerge, you cross the lane to climb the fence opposite (actually the footpath sign is slightly to the left but the hedge has grown to obscure this access and so people have taken the fence entry).

Now you must retrace your earlier route going to the right of the wall, over the stile, along the edge of the next field to a gate and stile then turning right to the wall-stile behind the church, and so back to the Copt Oak Inn.

Newton Burgoland
The Belper Arms

This strange-sounding place takes its name from the medieval Birgilon family which means Burgundian. The sign on the Belper Arms proclaims that this is the oldest pub in Leicestershire – 1290, but the outside setting is ordinary. It is the inside which startles and delights the visitor, for surely this is our dream pub realised. Low beams, nooks and crannies, pew-like seats, antiques in themselves, intricately decorated bench ends, chain-mail and shield on the walls, many small brass plates which each have a special message, pewter, pots, an upright piano and even a small museum – all these and more are contained in a twilight, slightly smoky atmosphere with roaring winter fires.

Then there is Uncle Fred or Five to Four Fred, the famous ghost. He is mentioned in the *British Book of Ghosts* and his presence is felt rather than seen. He does not like changes. When one landlord attempted an alteration he found himself short of breath, another was 'grabbed by the shoulder'. Fred likes women and seems to be returning to find a lost love. Women have reported 'bottom pinching' from out of thin air. Did he die in the old well reputed to be beneath the pub? There are ancient deeds showing that the pub was once called the Shepherd and Shepherdess but the name was changed in 1876 when Lord Belper owned the village – what would Fred think about that?

This freehouse has Marston's Pedigree and Adnams Best as well as changing guest beers and traditional ciders on draught. Drinking times are 12 noon-3 pm (Saturday 11.30 am-3 pm) and 6 pm-11 pm; all day on Sunday. There is a large garden at the rear with a children's adventure playground – plenty of room to run off excess energy. Children and dogs are welcome both inside and out, the latter on leads. There are excellent bar snacks as well as a full menu available 12 noon-2 pm and 6.30 pm-9.30 pm weekdays; on Sundays there is a traditional roast and bar food at lunchtime with food also available between 7 pm and 9 pm. The normal full menu is versatile and varied using fresh, local produce, with game and fish dishes a speciality.

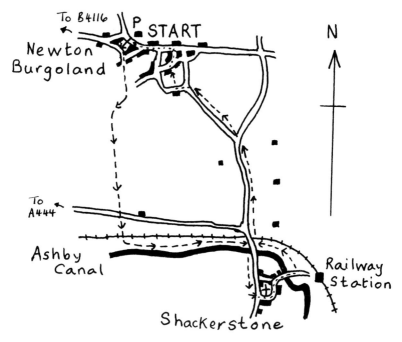

This is an outstanding pub and an exceptional walk which you must not miss!

Telephone: Measham (01530) 270530.

How to get there: Newton Burgoland is in north west Leicestershire and 6 miles away from Ibstock. Follow signs from the A447 to Odstone. You can also approach from junction 11 on the M42 via Appleby Magna and Snarestone or from the A444 turning right at Twycross onto the B4116.

Parking: There is a large car park at the pub and next to the main road. You can leave your car here if you prefer to take the walk first and drink afterwards.

Length of the walk: 4 miles. Maps: OS Landranger series 140, Pathfinder SK 20/30 (GR 370091).

This circular walk is over fairly level countryside. A wide and pleasant track leaves the village heading south to reach an old railway next to the Ashby Canal. You cross the line of the railway, now ploughed out on one side. Then you walk along the canal to Shackerstone, which means the village of the robbers. Here there is much to view, not only in the church and village, but also there is a fine castle site which you see as you cross bridge 53. The canal has a lovely bend here which is made more attractive by the long boats moored alongside. Go to Shackerstone railway station where there is a Railway Museum. Between Easter and the end of September steam trains run on the Battlefield Line to Market Bosworth and to the battlefield of Bosworth, where Richard III was slain in 1485 and the Middle Ages came to an end. You now return to Newton Burgoland via the country lane linking the two villages.

The Walk

From the pub car park cross to the footpath sign opposite. Pass through a small estate of modern houses and near a lamp post you see the way through onto a lane. Turn left and go about 100 yards to a bend. Here go straight ahead between Corner Farm and Drayton Fields Barn. Soon you reach a junction where a path from the village joins the one you are on. Keep straight on and follow a clear and wide grassy track which can get very muddy at times.

You pass through rather unspectacular countryside, generally flat. You will see yellow marker posts and blue arrows along the route. After you have walked about 1 mile you come to a wooden handgate. Go through this and keep to the right hand side of a large field. When you have crossed this field you arrive at a long straight lane running left to right in front of you. Cross straight over this, climb a small fence and go ahead for 100 yards to another tiny fence at the edge of a wood over the line of the old railway. In front of you see a spick and span sign pointing to Shackerstone. Now you are on the Ashby Canal towpath, at bridge 54. Turn left and follow the towpath to bridge 53 where a gate and stile take you onto the road. Turn right onto the bridge and look left for a good view of moored long boats and the castle site.

Carry on into the village. Turn left into Church Road and follow this round past the Rising Sun. Then turn right to cross a canal bridge and immediately left to walk on the towpath back to bridge 53. At this point you can divert to go to Shackerstone railway station if you wish, returning to bridge 53 to continue the walk.

From bridge 53 ascend to the road and turn left, going over the old railway bridge where you will see below that this is now a road leading to the station car park. Walk along the country lane until you reach a Y fork in ½ mile. Take the left fork and in another ½ mile, just before you reach Newton Burgoland, turn left into a narrow lane. On the right you see a footpath sign only 50 yards down the lane. Cross the stile here into the field towards the yellow marker post ahead. Go over another stile and follow a fenced path round to the village street. Turn right then left past the chapel (1807) into Dames Lane, then turn right to the main road. Here you turn left to return to the Belper Arms.

③⓪ **Appleby Magna**
The Black Horse

Clearly this is an ancient building, built in the early 17th century, but little seems to be known about its history. It is situated at the corner of Mawby's Lane and Top Street. As you enter the village from Snarestone it is one of the first buildings you see. The old beams and bowed walls indicate its age and inside, though there has been some modernisation, you can see the large old fireplace, now fitted with a stove, and the old beams. There is a lounge with a small dining room next door.

This is a Marston's house and Pedigree Bitter, Banks's Mild and Stella and Foster's lager are on sale with Strongbow Cider on draught. Drinking times are Monday to Saturday 12 noon-3 pm and 6 pm-11 pm, and Sunday 12 noon-10.30 pm. Food is obtainable between 12 noon-2.30 pm and 6.30 pm-9.30 pm every day except Sunday evenings. There is a wide range of food available, including traditional bar meals, steaks, fish, curries and vegetarian dishes. Although there is no garden, well-behaved dogs and children are welcome.

This is a pleasant pub which has the feel of a local rather than a fashionable rural retreat. It has great potential and is located in a most interesting, historic and attractive village.
Telephone: Measham (01530) 270588.

How to get there: Appleby Magna is about 5 miles south west of Ashby de la Zouch and a few miles away from Measham. Once remote on the far western boundary of Leicestershire, it is now only 1 mile from junction 11 on the M42, where the A444 crosses, aiming for Burton on Trent. A pleasant country approach is from Snarestone on the B4116.

Parking: There is a large car park behind the pub and you can leave your car there when you go on the walk.

Length of the walk: 4½ miles. Maps: OS Landranger series 140, Pathfinder SK 20/30 (GR 318098).

This walk is based on the Parish Walk prepared by the Parish Council of Appleby Magna and some villagers. The full leaflet can be obtained from local libraries and the Countryside Section of Leicestershire County Council. It is in the shape of a figure of eight starting at the Black Horse, passing the 15th century Moat House, the 1826 Baptist chapel, the remarkable Sir John Moore's Free School, thence proceeding to Appleby Parva, along Dingle Lane, under the M42 and returning via the ancient route known as Salt Street, Austrey Road, Appleby Parva and footpaths to your starting point. There are excellent views from the Salt Street ridge to the Derbyshire Hills, Lichfield Cathedral and to the east, Leicestershire's highest point, Bardon Hill. As you walk along you are very close to Staffordshire, Warwickshire and Derbyshire, in fact a county boundary follows Salt Street. Near here the area is named No Man's Heath as a sign of 'uncertainty' and it was a favoured place for prize fights where escape was possible if the law came along. One such incident was the Bendigo Thompson − Deaf Jem Burke fight in 1839.

The Walk

From the Black Horse turn left into Mawby's Lane and then turn left at the post office into the pathway leading past the Moat House. This is one of the best preserved medieval houses on a moated site in Leicestershire. According to Hoskins the original 15th century gatehouse 'still stands, practically unaltered, and behind is one of the best examples of black and white timber-framed houses in the county, dating probably from the middle of the 16th century and replacing the original manor house of the ancient Appleby family'. Look for the small dovecote on your right, towards the church. Turn left to join a footpath running from Church Street to Top Street. When